# A Classical Music Quiz
## with Richard Baker

*Devised and compiled by Roy Carter*

**DAVID & CHARLES**
Newton Abbot   London   North Pomfret (Vt)

**British Library Cataloguing in Publication Data**

Baker, Richard, b. 1925
    Richard Baker presents a musical quiz book.
    1. Music – Miscellanea
    I. Carter, Roy      II. Musical quiz book
    780'.76        ML63

    ISBN 0–7153–7819–8

Library of Congress Catalog Card Number: 80–67581

Printed in Great Britain
by Redwood Burn Ltd, Trowbridge & Esher
for David & Charles (Publishers) Limited
Brunel House Newton Abbot Devon

Published in the United States of America
by David & Charles Inc
North Pomfret Vermont 05053 USA

# Contents

# Introduction

There's a lot of fun to be had out of serious music, as I have discovered in the course of more than ten years as a panellist on the BBC TV music quiz *Face the Music*. On that programme, the most frequent kind of question required us to identify a fragment of music. You must have played that game unconsciously scores of time when you happen to hear a snatch of something on the radio, perhaps in the car, and you know it *so* well but just can't put a name to it. Then something distracts you when the programme presenter gives the title afterwards and you've missed it for ever. Maddening.

Of course, with a music quiz in book form, that's one kind of game you can't play. But it is amazing, as Roy Carter proves, how much entertainment can be derived from musical facts and figures. I have had a go at answering all the questions in this book, and I don't have to tell you how far I succeeded. What I am prepared to admit is that I learned a good deal in the process! I therefore recommend this book on two counts: it is enjoyable and educational in an entirely painless way.

The uses I foresee for this little volume are various. It will certainly beguile you on a solitary journey, for example, whoever you are. If you happen to be a student, you could use it as a pocket manual of musical general knowledge. But I also think it could provide the basis for setting up your own music quiz, at home with family or friends, or as a means of entertaining a larger audience at a fund-raising event. I have chaired such a home-made quiz on more than one occasion and I know how interesting and amusing they can be. Of course, a gramophone and/or a piano used in conjunction with the book would add greatly to the range of questions you can devise.

In whatever way you decide to use our music quiz, I am sure

you will find it interesting. Indeed, I believe it contradicts flatly the famous musician who said 'There are no good books on music'. There you are, I've started you off: who *did* say it?

Richard Baker

*April 1980*

(Answer: Sir Thomas Beecham. Quoted in *An Encyclopedia of Quotations about Music*, edited by Nat Shapiro, published by David & Charles.)

# 1

# Animal, Vegetable and Mineral

## Animals

1 Two well-known composers wrote pieces nicknamed *The Cat* and *Cat's Fugue* respectively. Who are the composers, and what are the compositions?
2 Can you name a piece by Chopin nicknamed *The Dog*?
3 Which of Joseph Haydn's compositions has the nickname *The Bear*?
4 Leoš Janáček composed an opera around a clever little beast. Which opera is this?
5 In a composition for piano by Franz Liszt designed as an *étude* and later revised as a symphonic poem for orchestra, the hero was lashed to a horse for a wild ride. Can you name the composition?
6 How many different members of the animal kingdom (including birds) are included in *Carnival of Animals* by Camille Saint-Saëns, and can you name them?

## Birds

1 Who composed a symphony nicknamed *The Hen*?
2 A Russian composer wrote an opera about a fabulous bird. Can you name the opera and its composer?
3 In a memorable recording of a popular orchestral work, each movement is prefaced by the verses of Ogden Nash, the American poet. Of one movement Nash writes: '. . . and she claims never to have heard of Pavlova.' What bird is Nash thinking about, and who composed the music?
4 What is 'The Hut on Fowl's Legs'?

5   Can you name a ballet by André Messager (1853–1929) which has strong bird connections?

6   In which descriptive Italian work does a recording of a night-ingale's song have to be used, and who was the composer?

## Children

1   Georges Bizet, Claude Debussy and Robert Schumann all wrote works that had children or childhood as their theme. What are the compositions?

2   Who composed *The Child and the Spells*, better known perhaps by its French title *L'enfant et les sortilèges*?

3   Which well-known opera has the names of a boy and a girl in the title?

4   Who wrote two suites entitled *Wand of Youth* and one called *Nursery Suite*?

5   Which twentieth-century English composer wrote the *Children's Overture*?

6   Who wrote the oratorio *A Child of our Time*?

## Colours

1   Can you name a symphony with four movements entitled 'Purple', 'Red', 'Blue' and 'Green'?

2   Who wrote *The Black Domino* Overture?

3   Who wrote the ballet *The Red Poppy*?

4   Who composed the piece *En blanc et noir* (*In Black and White*) for two pianos?

5   Which famous waltz, originally written for orchestra and chorus, extols one of Europe's major rivers

6   Who wrote the music for the film *The Red Pony*?

## Doctors of Music

Each of the doctors listed here features prominently in a work of music. Can you give the composer in each case, and also name the relevant work?

1 Doctor Gradus ad Parnassum.
2 Doctor Coppélius.
3 Doctor Miracle.
4 Doktor Faust.
5 Le docteur ox.
6 Doctor Falke.

## Fishy Stories

1 A famous composer wrote a song and a piano quintet with a well-known fish in the title. Who is the composer, and what is the song?
2 Claude Debussy named a piano composition, part of the *Images* for piano, after a species of freshwater fish. What is it called?
3 Who wrote *And God created Whales*, a composition using recordings of the sounds made by whales?
4 Who wrote *The Creel* for piano duet, basing it on *The Compleat Angler* by Isaac Walton?
5 From which country does the folk song *Cockles and Mussels* come?
6 Benjamin Britten composed a comic opera called *Albert. . .*?

## Flowers

1 Sergei Rachmaninov composed two songs named after flowers. What are they?
2 Here we are looking for a song by Mozart whose title is the name of a flower.
3 Which well-known Schubert song has a species of rose in its title?
4 In which opera does 'the presentation of the silver rose' occur?
5 Who composed a song with the title *Black Roses*?
6 On what kinds of musical instruments would you find 'roses'?

## Fruit

1 *Trois morceaux en forme de poire* (*Three Pieces in the Shape of a Pear*) were composed by whom, and for what instrument?
2 Which opera has the name of a citrus fruit in its title, and who wrote it?

3  His fairy dance was sugar-coated. Who is he, and where is the fairy to be found?
4  Who is Lily, the strawberry woman?
5  Which contemporary American composer created the electronic work *Silver Apples of the Moon*?
6  Who wrote the oratorio *Christ on the Mount of Olives*, op. 85?

## Gardens

All these clues should lead to answers containing the word 'garden' or 'gardens'.
1  Arnold Bax composed this symphonic poem in 1913. It relates to an Irish folk heroine, and in this case the garden in question is the sea.
2  An orchestral work by Delius first performed in 1909 but later revised and played in its new form in Edinburgh in 1913.
3  Another orchestral piece, by an Englishman who was born in 1875, died in 1959, and sometimes wrote under the pseudonym of Anton Vodorinski. His music was of a highly popular nature, but has since become unfashionable. The piece looked for here is probably the most popular that he ever wrote.
4  A piano composition by Debussy, written in 1903, which is no. 3 in his *Estampes*.
5  This great soprano was born in Aberdeen in 1877 and died there in 1967. Debussy chose her to create the role of Mélisande in his opera *Pelléas et Mélisande*. Making her début in 1900, she had marvellous acting ability and was an outstanding personality of her time.
6  A famous piece of music first written as a piano solo between 1908 and 1918 and later orchestrated by the composer in 1925 or thereabouts. Its composer, though Australian-born, later became a citizen of the United States; he was a fine pianist and achieved great prominence as an arranger of English folk-song themes.

## Golden Music

1  Dmitri Shostakovich wrote a ballet in three acts, first performed in 1930, which concerns the fight between Fascists and a Soviet football team. It was his first ballet score. Can you name this ballet, together with another by the same composer, both having the word 'golden' in their titles?

2  Can you name an oratorio by Sir Arthur Sullivan, based on a poem by Longfellow? It was first produced at the Leeds Festival in 1886.

3  Can you identify 'The Calf of Gold'?

4  Who wrote the *Golden* Sonata?

5  Which famous German opera concerns a treasure hidden at the bottom of a river, and from which series of operas does this work come?

6  A fantasy-opera by Nicolai Rimsky-Korsakov, based on a Russian fairy story as presented in a poem by Pushkin, was first produced in 1909. In 1934 a ballet version was produced which combines the arts of mime and dance and which is one of the most colourful spectacles on the ballet stage. The opera is not often performed today. Do you know what these works are called?

## Here Come the Boys

All these men's names are titles of operas—can you name the composer in each case?

1  L'Amico Fritz (Friend Fritz).   4  Siegfried.
2  Nerone (Nero).                  5  Rinaldo.
3  Edgar.                          6  Oberon.

## Here Come the Girls

Similarly, in this section, all the girls' names are titles of operas—can you name the composers?

1  Lulu.      4  Arabella.
2  Martha.    5  Daphne.
3  Norma.     6  Iris.

## I'll Drink to That

1 A well-known *brindisi* (drinking song) occurs in Act 1 of a famous opera by Verdi. It is sung by the hero Alfredo, and the chorus joins in after each measure. The aria is called 'Libiamo ne' lieti calici' ('Let us quaff from the wine cup o'erflowing'). What is the opera?

2 In Act 2 of this opera that redoubtable character Falstaff leads a spirited and famous drinking song at the *Gasthaus zum Hosenbande* (*Garter Inn*). The aria is called 'Als Bublein klein'. What is the opera, and who is the composer?

3 The basis of this drinking song by Verdi is subterfuge: the intention is to get one of the characters, Cassio, drunk. The aria, 'Inaffia l'ugola' ('Then let the cannikin clink'), is sung by one of the chief singers and occurs in Act 1. Can you name the opera, and who is the shady character leading the imbibing?

4 A one-act opera this time, and the *brindisi*—'Viva il vino spumeggiante' ('Hail the red wine richly flowing')—occurs towards the end of the work. It is sung by Turiddu, and is closely followed by the famous aria 'Mamma, quel vino è generoso' ('Mother, the red wine burns me like fire'), sung by the same character. What is the opera, and who wrote it?

5 Can you name the famous drinking song from Donizetti's *Lucrezia Borgia*, and do you know who sings it?

6 To end on a light note, here is an exhilarating Viennese opera. The aria 'Trinke, Liebchen, trinke schnell' is sung by Alfred, a singer by profession, in the first of the three acts. Although this is a famous drinking scene, the whole opera seems to overflow with champagne and bibulous activities! What is the opera and who is the composer?

## In the Countryside

1 What famous symphony has a first movement subtitled 'Pleasant feelings on arrival in the countryside'?

2 What is the name of the fourth in the set of symphonic poems by Bedřich Smetana entitled *Má Vlast* (*My Country*)?

3  Vaughan Williams's Symphony No. 3, composed in 1922, is entitled. . . ?

4  What is the subtitle of Beethoven's Piano Sonata No. 15 in D, op. 28?

5  In part three of Wagner's *Ring* Cycle—*Siegfried*—there is an orchestral interlude strongly descriptive of the countryside. Can you name the section?

6  In 1920 Arthur Honegger wrote an orchestral work splendidly evocative of the countryside. Can you give its name?

## Musical Jewels

Each of the pieces of music described here has one or more jewels in its title.

1  A famous soprano aria from Act 3 of Gounod's *Faust*.

2  An opera by Ermanno Wolf-Ferrari (1876–1948).

3  An overture by Daniel Auber (1782–1871).

4  An opera by Bizet.

5  An unfinished opera by Sir Arthur Sullivan, later completed by Sir Edward German.

6  A ballet, choreographed by Balanchine, using music by Fauré (*Pelléas et Mélisande* and *Shylock*), Stravinsky (Capriccio for piano and orchestra), and Tchaikovsky (Symphony No. 3 in D major). Inspired by precious stones such as emeralds, rubies and diamonds, it was first performed in 1967.

# 2
# Musicians

### Composer Last

Not all well-known composers began their working lives in the field of music. Can you name composers who had previously worked as:

1  A sailor?
2  A chemist?
3  A professional soldier?
4  A medical student?
5  A dentist?
6  A law student and civil servant?

### Composers

1  This German composer was born in 1809 and died in 1847. He wrote one of his most popular orchestral compositions at the age of seventeen and was a fine propagandist for the music of Bach. He became a friend of Queen Victoria and something of an idol of the Victorian musical public. One of his oratorios achieved immense popularity in England and is, even today, the only serious challenger Handel's *Messiah* has ever had. Can you name the composer and the oratorio?

2  This most 'French' of composers was actually born in Florence in 1633. He went to France at the age of thirteen, where he was employed as a kitchen-hand in the home of Mademoiselle de Montpensier. While entertaining the staff with his violin playing he was overheard by the Comte de Nogent, who secured his musical talents in *La Grande Bande* (the private orchestra of Louis XIV). He became known as the creator of French opera, introducing dramatic effects previously unknown. His best-known opera is *Armide et*

*Renaud*, but he also wrote ballets, symphonies and church music. Who was he?

3 'The most extraordinary and original musical genius that our country [England] has produced' (*Grove's Dictionary of Music and Musicians*). Born in Westminster in 1658, he was the son of an eminent musician (Gentleman of the Chapel Royal and Master of the Choristers at Westminster Abbey), received his musical training mostly under the tutorship of Dr John Blow, and became Composer-in-Ordinary to King Charles II at the age of only eighteen or nineteen. He composed operas, church works, sonatas, lessons for harpsichord and catches, and wrote music for over thirty dramatic works. His brother Daniel was also an excellent composer. He is buried in Westminster Abbey, where his memorial tablet is inscribed: 'Here lyes—Esq., who left this life, and is gone to that blessed place where only his harmony can be exceeded.' Who was he?

4 What are the first names of the following composers: Kodály (1882–1967); Buxtehude (1637–1707); Medtner (1880–1951)?

5 Who were known respectively as 'the Prince of Polyphony', 'the Poet of the Piano' and 'the Giant of the Oratorio'? Can you also supply these composers' dates?

6 This Viennese composer was a fellow pupil of Gustav Mahler at the Vienna Conservatory in approximately 1878. Considered by many to be second only to Schubert as a songwriter he composed something like five hundred songs and also wrote an opera and some instrumental pieces before dying in an asylum at the age of forty-three. Can you name the composer and his only completed opera?

### Composers on the Screen (1)

Which composer was played by the named actor in each of the following films?

1 Jean-Pierre Aumont in *Song of Scheherazade* in 1947.
2 Alan Badel in *Magic Fire* in 1956.
3 Carl Boehm in *The Magnificent Rebel* in 1960.

4  Richard Tauber in *Blossom Time* in 1934.
5  Fernand Gravet in *The Great Waltz* in 1938.
6  Richard Chamberlain in *The Music Lovers* in 1970.

## Composers on the Screen (2)

This time you are given the actor and the composer; can you name the film?

1  Jean-Louis Barrault as Berlioz in 1940.
2  Robert Powell as Mahler in 1975.
3  Toralf Maurstad as Grieg in 1970.
4  Maurice Evans as Sir Arthur Sullivan in 1953.
5  Paul Henreid as Schumann in 1947.
6  Robert Walker as Brahms in 1947.

## Cellists

1  When this famous cellist came upon the scene a new era began in the field of cello playing. Born in Tarragona, Spain, in 1876, by the time he was twelve he had played (and to a large extent mastered) nearly every orchestral instrument. He took up the cello seriously when he entered the Royal Conservatory of Barcelona; at a later date he was to direct his own orchestra there. In 1905 he formed, with the pianist Alfred Cortot and the violinist Jacques Thibaud, what was to become one of the finest chamber trios in the world. After the Spanish Civil War he exiled himself from Spain and made his home in Prades, where he held an annual festival from 1950. He spent some time in America, and gave concerts and recitals throughout the world. In 1956 he settled in Puerto Rico, where he died in 1973. Who was he?

2  Another eminent cellist was born in Russia in 1927. Initially he studied at the Moscow Conservatory under his father, making his début at the age of eight. He has had a distinguished concert career and has latterly concentrated more on conducting, though he is also a fine pianist and a talented composer. He is married to an equally famous Russian soprano and together they have given many notable recitals throughout the world. Can you name this cellist and his wife?

3 The subject of a famous portrait by Augustus John, this cellist was married to Pablo Casals from 1906 to 1912. She was born in Portugal in 1888 and died there in 1950. She studied in Leipzig, where she made a concert appearance under the baton of Arthur Nikisch, and was a pupil of Casals before marrying him. Her public début was made at the age of seventeen, and she soon won the highest international acclaim for her brilliant playing. She stayed in London for many years before returning to her native country. Who was she?

4 She was the daughter of a colonel in the Royal Engineers, born in north-west India in 1893 and brought to England at the age of three months. She studied at the Royal College of Music and with Hugo Becker at the Hochschule, Berlin. At the age of fourteen she became the first cellist and the youngest student to win the Mendelssohn International Prize, a competition open to both instrumentalists and singers. She was particularly well known for her performances of the concertos by Elgar and Delius dedicated to her, and of the solo sonata by Kodály. She had two sisters who were also musicians, but they never achieved her worldwide recognition. Who was she?

5 Probably the greatest of his time, he was born in Italy in 1822 and died there in 1901. He began to study his chosen instrument at the age of five, receiving tuition from his great-uncle Zanetti, an accomplished player and a very good teacher. He made his concert début at the age of fifteen, performing a concerto of his own composition. He travelled extensively, playing with musicians such as Liszt and Joachim, and became particularly well known in London, where he was a leading figure in the Monday and Saturday Popular Concerts of chamber music at St James's Hall. He was also a composer of some note, completing two cello concertos, a concertino, a number of fantasias and capriccios, and other pieces for cello, as well as vocal music. He edited six string sonatas by Boccherini, Locatelli and Marcello. His music has fallen from favour among present-day audiences, but as musician and artist he gained a reputation that has been equalled only by that of Pablo Casals. He commanded an unsurpassed technique, with great purity of tone, superb phrasing and perfect

intonation, that brought him the accolades not only of the public but also of his fellow artists. Who was he?

6 Born in Paris in 1906, he entered the Paris Conservatoire at the age of twelve and made his début at twenty-five. As a chamber player he made some memorable appearances with Schnabel and Szigeti as well as with Rubinstein and Piatigorsky. He is recognised throughout the world as a cellist of the highest standing. He has made frequent appearances with the leading orchestras of Europe and America and is now Professor of Cello at the Paris Conservatoire. Who is he?

## Conductors

1 This famous conductor was born in London in 1882 and trained at the Royal College of Music, later receiving his Bachelor of Music degree at Oxford University. He subsequently became organist of St James's, Piccadilly, and after a few years emigrated to America. He is best known for his work with the Philadelphia Orchestra, but he also conducted most of the major orchestras of the world. He appeared in three popular films, all with the Philadelphia Orchestra. He died in 1977. Who was he, and can you name the films?

2 Born in Westphalia in 1819, this child prodigy played the piano in public for the first time at the age of four. In 1836 he went to Paris to further his studies and spent much of his time in the company of Chopin, Liszt, Berlioz and Cherubini. In 1848 he settled in England, making Manchester his headquarters. The famous orchestra which bears his name was formed in 1857 and gave its first concert in 1858. He died in Manchester in 1895. Who was he?

3 Born in Lancashire in 1879, this conductor was the son of a wealthy businessman. He succeeded to his father's baronetcy in 1916, having himself been knighted previously for his services to music. He did not attend any formal music school. His first important concert was with the New Symphony Orchestra in 1906. As impresario, he introduced the Ballets Russes to London. He founded the London Philharmonic Orchestra in 1932, and in 1947 formed a second superb orchestra, the

Royal Philharmonic. He is associated particularly with the works of Mozart, Handel, Delius and a number of French composers, notably Berlioz. He died in 1961. Who was he?

4 Born in Berlin in 1879, he studied at the Stern Conservatory there and later became director of the Vienna Court Opera (1901–12). He appeared in England at a concert given by the Royal Philharmonic Society in 1909 and was such a success that he was immediately re-engaged for further concerts. He appeared frequently in England in the 1920s, particularly with the London Symphony Orchestra. In the 1930s he took a leading part in the establishment of the Salzburg Festival. When the Nazis came to power he moved to France, and from there to America, where he became a naturalised subject in 1946. His autobiography, *Theme and Variations*, was published in that year. Best known for his superb interpretation of the music of Mahler, Mozart and Schubert, he died in Manchester in 1962. Who was he?

5 He was one of the greatest conductors of all time. Born in Parma in 1867, he studied at the Conservatory there and in Milan; his instrument was the cello. Noted for his amazing memory, he deputised as conductor when he was with the orchestra of the Rio de Janeiro Opera: unknown to the audience, he conducted Verdi's *Aida* in its entirety, from memory. The performance was such a success that it led to engagements in Italy and other countries, and eventually he became chief conductor of La Scala, Milan, and of the Metropolitan in New York. In 1937 he formed the National Broadcasting Company's Symphony Orchestra, which he conducted for many years. His versatility was remarkable—he was equally at home with French impressionist music and Italian opera, and was an admirable interpreter of Sibelius, Wagner, Beethoven and Brahms. He died in 1957 but his legend lives on. Who was this remarkable conductor?

6 Born in Berlin in 1886, he began his musical education at the age of eight and later studied under Joseph Rheinberger and Max von Schillings. His first important conducting posts included the 'Tonkünstler' Orchestra of Vienna and the symphony concerts of the Berlin State Opera orchestra. He fol-

lowed the great Arthur Nikisch as conductor of the Leipzig
Gewandhaus concerts and also of the Berlin Philharmonic,
which he conducted from 1922 to 1945. One of the leading
musicians of his generation, he conducted frequently at the
Bayreuth and Salzburg festivals and was noted for his in-
terpretations of Wagner. His position of importance under
the Nazi regime in Germany aroused much controversy, but
in spite of this he was able to rebuild his career after the war.
He was also a fine interpreter of the music of Beethoven and
Bruckner; he died in 1954. Who was he?

## Pianists

1 He was born in Odessa in 1848 and died in 1933. Noted for his
interpretation of Chopin's music, only occasionally did he
play works by other composers such as Bach, Scarlatti,
Mendelssohn or Henselt. He was very eccentric and man-
nered, and frequently stopped in mid-performance to address
the audience on a variety of subjects—a whimsicality which
endeared itself to the public and became an attraction in itself.
Who was he?

2 This Polish pianist, composer and statesman was born in
Kurylowka in 1860 and died in New York in 1941. He wrote
an opera, a sonata, twelve songs and a symphony, but it is as a
pianist above all that he is remembered today. His pianistic
career was a continuous triumph. He made vast sums of
money, but as fast as he earned it he gave it away, helping
hundreds of artists in financial difficulties. He gave concerts
for the benefit of Jewish refugees from Nazi Germany, and
dedicated almost all his remaining money to the service of
Poland. He was made Prime Minister of Poland in 1919, and
received many of the highest decorations from various
countries of the world. He was a magnificent orator and a com-
passionate and warm human-being. What was his name?

3 Also a conductor, this famous pianist was born in Switzerland
in 1877 of French parentage. After studying with Decombes
(probably the last of Chopin's disciples) and Louis Diemer,
he became a foremost interpreter of Beethoven's concertos

and was subsequently appointed assistant conductor at Bayreuth. In 1905 he founded, with Jacques Thibaud and Pablo Casals, a trio that was to become world-renowned. He excelled in the interpretation of the Romantic School and in particular of the music of Chopin, having edited the *Études, Preludes* and *Ballades* in four volumes with valuable annotations. He also wrote several books on musical appreciation and technique, with particular reference to the art of pianoforte playing. He died in 1962. Who was he?

4 Famed as 'the greatest pianist that ever lived', he was born in Hungary in 1811 and died in Bayreuth in 1886. He learnt the piano at the age of six and gave his first public performance at the age of nine. His playing attracted the attention and admiration of Beethoven. As Kapellmeister (court musical director) in Weimar he was famous for the production of works by Wagner and Berlioz—it is no exaggeration to say that the merits of these composers were revealed to the world by this man. From 1859 to 1870 he lived mostly in Rome, where Pope Pius IX conferred on him the title of 'Abbé'. As a composer he is known as the father of the symphonic poem: his masterpieces in this genre include *Les Préludes, Tasso* and *Mazeppa*. He also composed concertos, rhapsodies, fantasies, *études*, etc, as well as producing brilliant paraphrases and transcriptions for pianoforte of operatic arias, Beethoven symphonies and so on. Who was he?

5 Born in Odessa in 1890, he studied—as did many other excellent pianists—with Leschetizky in Vienna. He made his début in England with great success in 1908. This was followed by a world tour with orchestral and recital appearances. He was noted for his Chopin playing, but his repertoire also included music by classical and other romantic composers. He became a naturalised British subject in 1937 and is best remembered by his many recordings made for HMV. He died in London in 1963. Who was he?

6 Born in Kiev in 1904, this pianist studied with Felix Blumenfeld and made his début at the age of seventeen. He later went to Paris and in 1928 played for the first time in America under the baton of Sir Thomas Beecham. In 1933, after becoming a

naturalised American subject, he married Toscanini's daughter Wanda. He retired from the concert platform for a period of twelve years, returning to it in 1965. He is without doubt one of the most technically accomplished and musically gifted pianists of our time. Who is he?

### Singers

1 One of the great coloratura sopranos of all time, she was born in Australia in 1861. Her real name was Helen Porter Armstrong (née Mitchell). She sang in public for the first time at the age of six. In 1886 she went to Paris to study under Madame Marchesi, making her brilliant début in Brussels a year later as Gilda in *Rigoletto*. Her reception at Covent Garden as Lucia in 1888 was equally rapturous. She appeared in all the most famous opera houses throughout the world, and as a reward for her extensive work in benefit concerts during World War I was created a Dame Commander of the British Empire. In 1926 she gave her famous gala 'farewell' at Covent Garden, appearing in scenes from her favourite operas. In 1929 she returned to her native Australia, where she died in 1931. Her famous stage name was derived from the city near to where she was born. Who was she?

2 This was the most popular tenor of his age. Born in Naples in 1873, he made his début in 1894; success came only gradually in Italy, though he was to create the tenor roles in Giordano's *Fedora*, Cilea's *Adriana Lecouvreur*, Franchetti's *Germania* and Puccini's *The Girl of the Golden West*. He appeared regularly at Covent Garden, his most successful role there being Rodolfo in *La Bohème*. His repertoire included more than fifty roles, mostly in Italian and French works. His voice was unique among the singers of his period in its combination of power and sweetness; his breath control was amazing, and his audiences used to marvel at the way in which he could deliver an extremely long phrase without ever conveying the suggestion of being at the end of his resources. Together with Nellie Melba he made the operas of Puccini popular in Britain. He probably contributed more than any other mu-

sician to the success of the gramophone, making over 150 gramophone records and cylinders. Apart from his singing activities, this tenor was also a cartoonist of some repute—a book of his drawings was published—and the composer of several popular songs. He died of pleurisy in 1921. Who was he?

3  Here is one of the finest baritones ever to appear on stage. He was born in Italy in 1857 and made his début in Donizetti's *La Favorita* in Rome in 1878. His technique was remarkable and his voice maintained its superb quality until he was nearly seventy. He was acclaimed throughout Europe and Russia, but sang infrequently at Covent Garden and, strangely, never at the Metropolitan Opera House in New York. His repertoire was vast, encompassing most of the baritone parts of classical Italian opera and Wolfram in *Tannhäuser*, but it was as Don Giovanni that he was especially hailed—his interpretation of Mozart was without peer in his time. He died near the town of his birth in 1928. Can you name this remarkable singer?

4  This eminent Russian bass was born in Kazan in 1873 and spent his childhood in poverty. At seventeen he joined a provincial opera company and in 1892 studied singing at Tiflis. He made his first appearance at Covent Garden in 1913 with the Russian company which, in that year, introduced Mussorgsky's *Boris Godunov* to England. That season also saw him in the same composer's *Khovantschina* and in Rimsky-Korsakov's *Ivan the Terrible*. The following year he added to these roles two parts in Borodin's *Prince Igor*. He made extensive tours in America, raising a great deal of money to help his famine-stricken countrymen, and was engaged regularly at the Chicago Opera and at the Metropolitan Opera in New York from 1921 to 1925. This marvellous singer died in Paris in 1938. Who was he?

5  Born in Lancaster, England, in 1912, this contralto originally studied as a pianist and did not take singing lessons until 1940. She was a pupil of Roy Henderson and made her operatic début in the title role of Britten's *Rape of Lucretia* in 1946. Her international reputation was of the highest order and she was, without doubt, the finest contralto of her time. Although she

appeared in other operas, such as Gluck's *Orfeo ed Euridice*, her principal activities were confined to the concert hall, where she was much admired as an interpreter of the music of Brahms and Mahler. Especially acclaimed was her collaboration with Bruno Walter in Mahler's song cycles, and particularly *Das Lied von der Erde* (*The Song of the Earth*). A fatal illness curtailed her illustrious career, and she died in 1953 at the early age of forty-one. Who was this great singer?

6 Her full name was Cecilia Sophia Anna Maria Kalogero-poulos, and she was born of Greek parents in the United States in 1923. She studied singing at the Conservatory in Athens, where her teacher was the celebrated Elvira de Hidilgo, and she made her début there in 1938 as Martha in d'Albert's *Tiefland*. In 1947 she made her first Italian appearance at Verona as La Gioconda in the opera by Ponchielli. That same year she married a wealthy manufacturer, Signor Meneghini. She sang regularly at La Scala, Milan, and established a reputation as the finest dramatic soprano of her day. She was unique in her command of style and dramatic ability. Her appearances always generated excitement and once on the stage she held the audience spellbound. Her vocal technique, although by no means flawless, was robust and penetrating, with superb diction. It was in the *bel canto* period of opera that she excelled, particularly in the works of Bellini and Donizetti and also operatic composers such as Puccini and Verdi. In 1960 she retired from the operatic stage, although she made several more concert appearances, with varying success. She died in Paris in 1977, and it will undoubtedly be many years before her manifold achievements are rivalled. Who was she?

### Violinists

1 The son of another distinguished violinist, this musician was born in Russia in 1901. In 1910 he was the youngest student in Leopold Auer's class at the Imperial Conservatory in St Petersburg, and at the age of twelve he made his concert début touring Russia, Germany and Scandinavia, with outstanding

success. After the Russian Revolution he emigrated to America, becoming naturalised in 1925. He won the reputation of a superb performer, both technically and musically, and his many gramophone records are a testament to his art. He has commissioned a number of fine works from living composers, including the Walton concerto. Although he still performs, his appearances are becoming less frequent. Who is he?

2 The son of a poor shopkeeper, this famous violinist first played in public at the age of eleven. He was born in Genoa in 1782 and died in Nice in 1840. In his late teens he ran away from home and started concert touring on his own account, remaining in Italy until 1828, during which time he aroused unbounded enthusiasm. He then visited Vienna, Berlin, Paris and London, amassing a fortune in the process, and eventually retired. As a soloist he was the most wonderful and original of players; his technique was incredible, and, combined with his eccentricities, tricks of virtuosity and dazzling genius, made him 'the wonder of the age'. As a composer he wrote violin concertos, studies for the violin, string quartets with guitar, twelve sonatas for violin and guitar and concert pieces for violin and orchestra. Who was this extraordinary man?

3 This much-loved violinist was born in Vienna in 1875 and died in New York in 1962. He studied at the Vienna Conservatory under Hellmesberger and Auer, and also at the Paris Conservatoire with Massart and Delibes. Well known for his stylishness, virtuosity and musicality, he toured Europe and America with tremendous success on many occasions, and long held a leading position amongst the world's great violinists. In addition, he composed many popular small pieces for his instrument: a number of these were adaptations of Viennese folk melodies; the bulk were attributed to little-known composers of the past, but in 1935 he announced that they were in fact his own compositions. Who was he?

4 Over the past two decades this violinist has also appeared frequently as a conductor. He was born in New York in 1916, began his musical studies at the age of four and made his concert début in San Francisco at the age of seven, subse-

quently creating a furore as a prodigy in all parts of the world. He studied with Georges Enesco in Paris, where his first public performance was given with the Lamoureux Orchestra. Further European conquests included the remarkable achievement of playing Bach, Beethoven and Brahms violin concertos all in one evening, conducted by Bruno Walter. His recording of the Elgar Violin Concerto, made at the age of sixteen, remains one of the classic gramophone recordings of all time. He went on to make hundreds of records, and happily continues to make music of many kinds as violinist, viola player and conductor. He has lived in London for many years. Who is he?

5   This eminent player was born near Pressburg in 1831. He began his violin studies at the age of five, entered the Vienna Conservatory at ten and made his concert début at twelve, with great success. Leipzig was his home until 1849, where he enjoyed the friendship of Schumann, Mendelssohn and David. In 1854 he accepted the position of conductor of concerts and solo violinist to the King of Hanover. His style of playing, nurtured on the best classical models, was remarkable for its dignity, breadth and flawless technical mastery, winning for him the title of 'King of Violinists'. Who was this king?

6   This celebrated modern violinist was born in Odessa in 1908 and died in Amsterdam in 1974. Beginning his studies at the age of five, he subsequently entered Odessa Conservatory, from which he graduated at the age of eighteen, winning a number of prizes including the Brussels competition of 1937. From 1934 onwards he taught at the Moscow Conservatory, becoming known to the world as a performer only after World War II. He gave the first performances of concertos by Miaskovsky, Khatchaturian and Shostakovich, and is survived by a son whose career to date has almost equalled the brilliance of his father's. Can you name this illustrious pair?

## Wagner

1 Here are three famous Wagner characters; can you fit them into their respective operas? Wolfram von Eschenbach; Daland; Kurwenal.

2 Similarly can you name the operas in which these female characters apppear? Elsa of Brabant; Elizabeth; Eva.

3 There is a plaque on a house in Switzerland which reads (in translation):

> Richard Wagner
> lived in this house
> from April 1866 to April 1872.
> Here he completed *Die Meistersinger,*
> *Siegfried, Götterdämmerung, Beethoven,*
> *Kaisermarsch, Siegfried-Idyll*

Where is the house, and what is its significance today?

4 Can you spot the odd one out of these three Wagner operas, and say why? *Die Hochzeit; Die Feen; Das Liebesverbot, oder Die Novize von Palermo.*

5 In 1830 Wagner made an arrangement for pianoforte of a famous work by Beethoven. Can you name the work?

6 Apart from the preludes/overtures to the famous music dramas, how many overtures (including concert overtures) did Wagner write?

## With a Little Help from my Friends

All the works listed below were either composed for one instrument and later orchestrated by another composer, or were sketched, as it were, by the composer and then orchestrated by a pupil or enthusiast. Can you say what the change was in each case, and name the arrangers involved?

1 Carl Maria von Weber: *Invitation to the Dance.*

2 Johann Sebastian Bach: Toccata and Fugue in D minor.

3 Modeste Mussorgsky: *Pictures from an Exhibition.*

4 Gabriel Fauré: incidental music to *Pelléas et Mélisande.*

5 Claude Debussy: *Petite Suite.*

6 Johannes Brahms: Piano Quartet in G minor.

## Women Composers

Here are clues to the identity of six women composers. Who are they, and can you supply the names of their best-known works?

1  Her father was a celebrated architect and her husband a conductor and specialist in contemporary music.
2  Less well known than her celebrated sister, though she was the first woman to win the Prix de Rome.
3  A rather formidable character who, though English, had her first and greatest success in Germany.
4  The odd one out in a famous group of French composers.
5  A Polish composer with a name very similar to that of a male compatriot and fellow composer.
6  Possibly the first American woman to achieve fame as a composer of serious music.

# 3

# Quick General Musical Knowledge Quiz

How many questions can you answer in half an hour?

1 Beethoven dedicated a symphony to Napoleon. Which one—and which key is it in?

2 How many symphonies did Haydn write?

3 Who is the odd man out here: Paderewski; Leschetizky; Wieniawski; Godowsky?

4 Name three English composers whose surnames begin with the letter 'A'.

5 Name any three composers whose surnames begin with the letter 'Z'.

6 What do these abbreviations stand for: LTCL; LGSM?

7 Who composed the *Abegg* Variations, and what is the significance of their title?

8 Who composed 'The Flight of the Bumblebee', and from what work does it come?

9 For what were the Amati family of Cremona famous?

10 What was Bartolommeo Cristofori's contribution to music?

11 Johann the elder, Johann the younger, Joseph and Eduard were all members of which famous Austrian family?

12 Under what pseudonym did the music critic Philip Heseltine compose?

13 What is remarkable about the cast of Puccini's one-act opera *Suor Angelica*?

14 What is a glass harmonica?

15 An American composer, born in 1916, composed a Symphony No. 5½. Who is he?

16 Who is known as 'the father of Swedish music'?

17 Which twentieth-century composer named a work after an American railway engine? Can you name the work?

18  Who wrote the opera *Mozart and Salieri*?
19  What is the *Hexameron*?
20  Who composed *Rule, Britannia*?
21  Who wrote *The Game of Cards*, often known as *The Card Party*, in three deals?
22  Who wrote the opera *The Queen of Spades*?
23  What is a serpent?
24  Who wrote *A Lincoln Portrait*?
25  Who wrote *Five Tudor Portraits*?
26  Who composed a symphony to be played on the march?
27  What is the difference between a baryton and a baritone?
28  How many sons did Johann Sebastian Bach have?
29  What is the meaning of the Italian term *animato*?
30  What is a gemshorn?
31  What is an oliphant?
32  What is a *zarzuela*?
33  Apart from being among the world's finest pianists, what other musical occupation is followed by Daniel Barenboim and Vladimir Ashkenazy?
34  Who composed a remarkable forty-part motet entitled *Spem in Alium*?
35  What have *Rio Grande* by Constant Lambert and *La Création du monde* by Darius Milhaud in common?
36  Can you complete these famous pairs of duo pianists: Phyllis Sellick and ?; Ethel Bartlett and ?; Vitya Vronsky and ?
37  What are a *caña*, a *zapateado* and a *jota*?
38  Who is the odd man out: Eugène Ysaÿe, Jan Kubelik, Fritz Kreisler, Pablo Casals?
39  Who was Alessandro Longo?
40  What are 'hairpins'?
41  Which composer appears on the current (1980) ten-franc note in France?
42  Who wrote the opera *The Barber of Baghdad*?
43  Who wrote the opera *The Caliph of Baghdad*?
44  Who was Ludwig von Köchel?
45  Who perfected the twelve-tone system?
46  What is the *Ghost* Trio?
47  What was Manuel de Falla's last (unfinished) work?

48 Who wrote *Schelomo, Israel* Symphony and *Baalshem*?

49 Can you name the three works making up the Carl Orff trilogy known collectively as *Il Trionfo*?

50 Who wrote a Prelude and Fugue on the Name of BACH?

51 What is a *Heldentenor*?

52 What are *Lieder*?

53 What is the difference between a coloratura and a lyric soprano?

54 What is a counter-tenor?

55 What is the name given to the deepest human voice?

56 'The Lass that Loved a Sailor' is the subtitle of which opera by Gilbert and Sullivan?

57 What are the subtitles of Gilbert and Sullivan's *The Mikado* and *The Grand Duke*?

58 Who composed the following operas: *Hugh the Drover* (1924), *Sir John in Love* (1929), *The Poisoned Kiss* (1936) and *Riders to the Sea* (1937)?

59 Can you name the composers of these three Russian operas: *Lady Macbeth of Mtsensk* (1934); *Ivan the Terrible* (1873); *Russlan and Ludmilla* (1842)?

60 Who used the pseudonym Paul Klenovsky when orchestrating Bach's famous Toccata and Fugue in D minor?

61 What was the full name of Edward German, known for light operas such as *Merrie England, Tom Jones* and *Nell Gwynne*, and for his dances for Shakespeare's *Henry VIII*?

62 Which composer employed anvils, motor horns, aeroplane propellers and electric bells in one of his compositions?

63 What unusual effect did Richard Strauss use in both his *Don Quixote* and his *Alpine Symphony*?

64 Who introduces, in one of his operas, a military band, an out-of-tune piano and an accordion?

65 Who composed *The Age of Gold*?

66 Who composed *Mozartiana* (Suite No. 4 for orchestra)?

67 Who composed *Scarlattiana* for piano and orchestra?

68 What do the initials ISCM stand for?

69 Can you name three works in which the British national anthem is used?

70 Who wrote the orchestral rhapsody *España*?

71  Who wrote the waltz *España*?
72  Who wrote the *Goldberg* Variations?
73  Who wrote the *Golden* Sonata?
74  What is Baroque music?
75  Who is Barraqué?
76  Who transcribed for piano Berlioz's *Symphonie fantastique*?
77  Who composed the opera *Palestrina*?
78  Who composed the *Missa Papae Marcelli* (*Mass of Pope Marcellus*)?
79  Who composed 'Four Serious Songs' ('Vier ernste Gesänge')?
80  Who composed Four Sacred Pieces?
81  Who composed the symphonic poem *The Ballad of Reading Gaol*?
82  What do the composers Louis Gottschalk (1829–69), Samuel Coleridge-Taylor (1875–1912) and Chevalier St George (1745–99) have in common?
83  Who composed the cantata, op. 102, *The American Flag*?
84  Who composed a work entitled *New York Profiles*?
85  What is the difference between a vihuela and a viola?
86  Chopin wrote a set of piano variations on an aria from a Mozart opera. Can you name the aria and the opera?
87  Which composer was also a railway freight officer?
88  Who wrote *Poem of Ecstasy* and *Poem of Fire*?
89  Name two composers who wrote music connected with Belshazzar's Feast.
90  From which work does 'The Swan of Tuonela' come?
91  Who wrote *Swan White*?
92  Who wrote the popular piano piece *Rustle of Spring*?
93  Who wrote the operas *The Wreckers* and *The Boatswain's Mate*?
94  Who was John Taverner?
95  Who is John Tavener?
96  Who wrote the suite *Through the Looking-Glass*?
97  Who wrote the suite *Don Quichotte*?
98  Who wrote *Don Quixote*, fantastic variations, op. 35?
99  Who wrote Italian Serenade?
100 Who wrote Italian Caprice?

# 4

# Art, Literature and Music

## Art and Music

1 Which composer was inspired by a painting by Arnold Böcklin (1827–1901) to write a symphonic poem, and what is the name of the work, which has the same name as the painting?

2 Ten paintings by a rather obscure Russian artist inspired Mussorgsky to compose a famous piano work, which was later orchestrated by a French composer. Can you name the work, the French composer and the painter?

3 A Spanish composer named a set of piano pieces and later an opera after an artist whom he greatly admired. Can you name the composer, the composition and the artist?

4 This composer expressed in music three paintings by a famous Italian artist of the early sixteenth century. Who was the composer and what is the name of the work (its title will give you the name of the artist)?

5 Another early sixteenth-century painter, Grünewald, inspired compositions by a modern German composer who died in 1963. Can you name the composer and the work?

6 Which contemporary British composer paid tribute to a great modern Russian-born painter, and what was the name of the work?

## The Bible

1 Who composed the 'Biblical Songs', op. 99?
2 Who composed *Job*, a masque for dancing?
3 Who composed an oratorio entitled *The Creation*?
4 What is *Moses and Aaron*, and who composed it?

5 Which seventeenth-century German composer wrote 'Six Biblical Sonatas'?
6 Who wrote the *Jeremiah* Symphony?

## May I Have a Programme?

Here are six well-known works, each of which has a programme that is familiar to most concert-goers. Can you identify each work from the synopsis and name the composer?

1 In this famous orchestral work by an equally famous Frenchman, a woman performs a solo dance on a table. She is surrounded by an audience of men who follow her movements and emotions with lascivious stares. As she grows more and more animated, their excitement increases. They clap their hands, pound their heels in accompaniment and finally, at the moment of a change of key, draw their knives and a violent tavern brawl ensues.

2 Originally a descriptive piano piece, it was first performed in Paris in a revised and orchestrated form on 14 April 1872. The score of this work bears the following introduction by the composer: 'The subject of this symphonic poem is feminine seduction, the triumphant battle of weakness against strength. The spinning wheel is only a pretext, chosen only because of its rhythm and the general character of the piece.'

3 Originally scored for piano and orchestra, this composition was later revised by the composer. The best-known version, however, is undoubtedly by Rimsky-Korsakov, who headed his edition of the score with this outline: 'Subterranean sounds of supernatural voices—appearance of the spirits of darkness, followed by Satan himself—glorification of Satan and celebration of the Black Mass—the Sabbath Revels—at the height of the orgies the bell of the village church, sounding in the distance disperses the spirits of darkness—daybreak.'

4 This is the best-known work of a musical giant who gives the listener the following programme note: 'A young musician of morbidly sensitive temperament and fiery imagination poisons himself with opium in a fit of lovesick despair. The dose of the narcotic, too weak to kill him, plunges him into a

deep slumber, in which his sensations, his emotions, his memories are transformed in his sick mind into musical thoughts and images. The loved one herself has become a melody to him, an *idée fixe* as it were, that he encounters and hears everywhere. He dreams that he has killed his beloved, that he is condemned to death. He sees himself at the Sabbath in the midst of a frightful troop of ghosts, sorcerers, monsters of every kind who come together for his funeral.'

5 This colourful tone poem was composed in 1924. Its four movements are described as follows in the printed score: 'Children are at play in the pine groves of the Villa Borghese, dancing the Italian equivalent of *Ring-a-Ring-a-Roses*. They mimic marching soldiers and battles; they chirp with excitement like swallows at evening. Suddenly the scene changes. And we see the shadows of the pines, which crown the entrance of a catacomb. From the depths rises a dolorous chant, which spreads solemnly, like a hymn, and then mysteriously dies away. There is a tremor in the air. The pines of Janiculum Hill are profiled in the full moon. A nightingale sings. Misty dawn on the Appian Way. Solitary pines stand guard over the tragic campagna. The faint, unceasing rhythm of numberless steps. A vision of ancient glories appears to the poet's fantasy. Trumpets blare and a consular army erupts, in the brilliance of the newly risen sun, towards the Sacred Way, mounting to a triumph on the Capitoline Hill.'

6 When the composer of this tone poem sent the score to his publisher he appended the following outline of what his composition depicted: 'Two springs pour forth their streams in the shade of the Bohemian forest, the one warm and gushing, the other cold and tranquil, their waves, joyfully flowing over rocky beds, unite and sparkle in the rays of the morning sun. The forest brook rushing on, becomes the River Vltava. Coursing through Bohemia's valleys it grows into a mighty stream. It flows through dense woods from which come joyous hunting sounds, and the notes of the hunter's horn drawing ever nearer and nearer.

'It flows through emerald meadows and lowlands, where a wedding feast is being celebrated with songs and dancing. By night in its glittering waves, wood and water nymphs hold their revels. And these waters reflect many a fortress and castle—witnesses of a bygone age of knightly splendour, and the martial glory of days that are no more. At the rapids of St John the stream speeds on, winding its way through cataracts and hewing a path for its foaming waters through the rocky chasm into the broad riverbed, in which it flows on in majestic calm toward Prague, welcomed by time-honoured Vyšehrad, to disappear in far distance from the poet's gaze.'

## Drama

1 Can you name three composers and the orchestral works by them that are associated with Shakespeare's *Romeo and Juliet*—one of which has solo and choral voices?
2 *Hamlet* has inspired several composers. Can you name three of them and the orchestral works associated with the play?
3 Who composed the incidental music to a famous play by Henrik Ibsen, and can you name the play?
4 Can you name three composers of music for Maurice Maeterlinck's play *Pelléas et Mélisande*?
5 Which three composers have written music associated with the legend of Prometheus?
6 On which novel did Verdi base his opera *La Traviata*?

## Fairy Tales

1 What are *skazki*, and can you name two composers who used the word in the titles of their compositions?
2 This Russian ballet is based on a popular Russian fairy tale. It has been scored by two composers: Cesare Pugni (1802–70) wrote the music for the production at the Bolshoi in St Petersburg in 1864, while Rodion Shchedrin (b. 1932) composed an entirely new score for the production at the Bolshoi in Moscow in 1960. Can you name this charming ballet?
3 Two composers have written operas with the title *Cinderella*. Can you name them?
4 Who composed the music for the ballet *Cinderella*, op. 87, op. 107 and op. 108?

5 The ballet *The Prince of the Pagodas* is based on a French fairy tale. Who composed the music?
6 In which ballet will you find Cinderella and her Prince, Puss-in-Boots, Little Red Riding Hood and Hop-o-my-Thumb?

### Films

Which well-known composer wrote the music for the following films?
1 *The Sea Hawk*, starring Errol Flynn (1940).
2 *The Louisiana Story*, a documentary film (1940).
3 *The Overlanders*, starring Chips Rafferty (1946).
4 *Things to Come*, starring Ralph Richardson and Raymond Massey (1936).
5 *The First of the Few*, starring Leslie Howard (1942).
6 *Scott of the Antarctic*, starring John Mills (1948).

### Just a Few Lines...

Here are letters from three famous composers. Can you name the writers?

1 To: The Margrave of Brandenburg

My Lord,

As I had the good fortune a few years ago to be heard by your Royal Highness, at Your Highness's command, as I noticed that your Highness took some pleasure in the little talents which Heaven has given me for Music, and as in taking leave of Your Royal Highness, Your Highness deigned to honour me with the command to send Your Highness some pieces of my composition: I have in accordance with Your Highness's most gracious orders taken the liberty of rendering my most humble duty to Your Royal Highness with the present concertos, which I have adapted to several instruments; begging Your Highness most humbly not to judge their imperfection with the rigour of that discriminating and sensitive taste, which everyone knows him to

have for musical works, but rather to take into benign consider-
ation the profound respect and the most humble obedience
which I thus attempt to show Him. For the rest, my Lord, I
humbly beg Your Royal Highness to have the goodness to continue Your Royal Highness's gracious favour toward me, and to
be assured that nothing is so close to my heart as the wish that I
may be employed on occasions more worthy of Your Royal
Highness and of Your Royal Highness's service—I, who with
unparalleled zeal am, my Lord,

Your Royal Highness's
Most humble and most obedient servant,

*Cöthen, 24 March 1721*


## 2  To: Hector Berlioz

My dear friend,

Since the death of Beethoven, none but Berlioz has been able to
make him live again; and I, who have savoured your divine compositions, worthy of the genius that you are, feel it my duty to beg
you to accept, as a token of my homage, twenty thousand francs,
which will be remitted to you by the Baron Rothschild on presentation of the enclosed. Believe me your most affectionate friend,
signed,

*Paris, 18 December 1838*


## 3  To: Joseph Haydn at Eisenstadt

To my dear friend Haydn,

A father who had decided to send out his sons into the great
world, thought it his duty to entrust them to the protection and
guidance of a man who was very celebrated at the time and who,
moreover, happened to be his best friend.

   In like manner I send my six sons to you, most celebrated and
very dear friend. They are, indeed, the fruit of a long and la-
borious study; but the hope which many friends have given me

that this toil will be in some degree rewarded, encourages me and flatters me with the thought that these children may one day prove a source of consolation to me. During your last stay in this capital you yourself, my very dear friend, expressed to me your approval of these compositions, your good opinion encourages me to offer them to you and leads me to hope that you will not consider them wholly unworthy of your favour. Please then receive them kindly and be to them a father, guide and friend! From this moment I surrender to you all my rights over them. I entreat you, however, to be indulgent to those faults which may have escaped a father's partial eye, and, in spite of them, to continue your generous friendship towards one who so highly appreciates it. Meanwhile, I remain with all my heart, dearest friend, your most sincere friend,

*Vienna, 1 September 1785*

## Literature and Music

1 Who composed the symphonic poem *Egdon Heath*, and what literary work inspired its composition?
2 Can you name two composers who were inspired by Byron's dramatic poem *Manfred*?
3 Name two English composers who wrote song cycles based on works by A. E. Housman?
4 Which composer wrote a song cycle entitled *In a Persian Garden*, and on what famous book of poems is it based?
5 Who composed the cantata trilogy *Hiawatha*, and who wrote the poem that inspired it?
6 Who composed *The Creation*. What were the two sources of the text, which was translated into German? What is the German title?

## Myths and Legends

1 Which composer wrote four symphonic poems, op. 22, called *Legends*, which are based on the Finnish national saga Kalevala, and can you name the four *Legends*?

2 Liszt wrote *Deux Légendes* for piano in 1866. He also wrote two oratorios with the word 'legend' in the title. Can you name the two legends for piano and the oratorios?

3 Richard Strauss wrote two ballets. The second of these, *Schlagobers* (*Whipped Cream*), was written in 1921. Can you name the first?

4 Which twentieth-century composer wrote a ballet, scored for strings only, that is 'founded on moments or episodes in Greek mythology plastically interpreted by dancing of the so-called classical school', and can you name the ballet?

5 Who wrote an opera called *The Olympians*?

6 Which two of Offenbach's tuneful and delightful operettas feature characters from the Greek myths in their titles?

## Poets' Corner

The following lines all relate to music. Can you name both the author and the work from which they are taken?

1 Music to hear, why hear'st thou music sadly?

2 From harmony, from heavenly harmony
This universal frame began.

3 There let the pealing organ blow,
To the full voiced choir below.

4 They talked of their concerts and singers and scores,
And pitied the fever that kept me indoors.

5 Music when soft voices die,
Vibrates in the memory—

6 Oh Galuppi, Baldassaro, this is very sad to find!
I can hardly misconceive you; it would prove me deaf and
blind.

## Sir Walter Scott and Opera

Can you name the titles of operas based on the following works by Sir Walter Scott?

1 *Guy Mannering* and *The Monastery*.

2 *Ivanhoe*.

3 *The Bride of Lammermoor*.

4 *Old Mortality*.
5 *St Valentine's Day*.
6 *The Lady of the Lake*.

## Witches, Goblins and Fairies

1 Can you name the symphonic poem, op. 108, by Dvořák that has a rather ominous title?

2 On an aquatic note, can you name Dvořák's symphonic poem, op. 107?

3 What is the title of the fifth movement of Berlioz's *Symphonie fantastique*?

4 Which opera by Purcell was adapted from Shakespeare's *A Midsummer Night's Dream*?

5 Philip Heseltine (1894–1930) was an eminent British composer who wrote over eighty songs. Amongst his works are *Three Dirges by Webster*, the song cycle, *The Curlew, An Old Song, Corpus Christi* and *Sorrow's Lullaby*, but his best known composition is the *Capriol* Suite, which is based on French popular songs and dances of the sixteenth century. He is better known by his *nom de plume*. Do you know it?

6 Do you know the name of the ballet by Stravinsky, first performed in 1928 at the Paris Opéra by Rubinstein's company, which was based on *The Ice Maiden* by Hans Anderson?

# 5
# Faraway Places

### Capital Cities

1 Which composer wrote about the fountains and pines of the eternal city, and can you name the works?
2 Can you identify the composer and complete the title of: ——*The Song of a Great City*?
3 Who wrote an overture to celebrate a city's festival in 1956, and can you name the work?
4 A Symphony No. 38 had the name of a city applied to it after the first performance had been given there in 1787. Can you name the city and the composer?
5 Can you name a waltz and subsequent operetta compiled from music by a famous son that extols the virtues of his city, and who was the composer?
6 Can you name an organ work by a French composer, which is based on the chimes of Big Ben in London?

### First Produced in London

Can you name the composer of the incidental music to the following plays and also, if possible, the London theatre in which they were first produced and give the date of their first production?
1 *Johnson over Jordan* by J. B. Priestley.
2 *Where the Rainbow Ends* by Clifford Mills and John Ramsey.
3 *The Starlight Express* by Violet Pearn, adapted from Algernon Blackwood's novel *A Prisoner in Fairyland*.
4 *Pelléas et Mélisande* by Maurice Maeterlinck.
5 *Hassan* by James Elroy Flecker.
6 *The Ascent of F6* by W. H. Auden and Christopher Isherwood.

## Folk Songs and Dances in Music

1 Which well-known Russian folk song did Tchaikovsky use in his Symphony No. 4?

2 Alexander Glazunov used a well-known Russian folk song in a symphonic poem composed in 1884. What is it?

3 Georges Bizet incorporated a well-known Provençal dance rhythm in the incidental music to a play. What is the dance, who wrote the play and what is its title?

4 Can you name four Spanish composers who used traditional Spanish folk songs and dances in their works?

5 Who composed the English Folk Song Suite and for what medium?

6 Which composer, born in Australia, collected and edited English folk music, and incorporated a large quantity in his own compositions?

## España

The titles of these six works all have a Spanish connection, but none of them was written by a Spaniard. Can you name their composers?

1 *Symphonie Espagnole*, op. 21.

2 *L'Heure Espagnole* (*The Spanish Hour*).

3 *Rapsodie Espagnole* (*Spanish Rhapsody*).

4 *España*.

5 *Capriccio Espagnol*, op. 34 (*Spanish Caprice*).

6 *The Spanish Lady*.

## Heavenly Music

The answers to the following questions refer to heavenly bodies. Can you name them?

1 Lord Gerald Hugh Tyrwhitt-Wilson Berners (1883–1950) was a diplomat, painter and author, as well as a composer. Can you name the ballet he wrote, which had a scenario by Sacheverell Sitwell?

2 Gustav Holst's op. 32 is well known, but can you name all the movements as well as the work itself?

3 One of the most famous tenor arias translates into English as 'The stars were brightly shining'. Do you know what the title is in the original Italian, and from which opera it comes?

4 What nickname is given to Mozart's Symphony No. 41 in C major, K. 551?

5 Which famous English novel was adapted as an opera by John Linton Gardner (b. 1917)?

6 Of more than 283 works by a certain composer, the waltz, op. 235, is perhaps his most popular composition. Can you name the work and the composer, who was an architect before becoming a successful musician?

## London

1 Sir Edward Elgar wrote an exhilarating concert overture, evocative of Cockneys and London, subtitled 'In London town'. Can you name the work?

2 What are known as the 'London Symphonies', and who composed them?

3 Who composed the *St Paul's Suite*?

4 One of this composer's most popular suites contains the movements: 'Covent Garden', 'Westminster' and 'Knightsbridge'. The suite was so successful that he composed a second with the movements: 'Oxford Street', 'Langham Place' and 'Mayfair'. Can you name the composer and the two suites?

5 Which composer was, in his early college life, closely associated with the Sitwell family, collaborating with one of them in what was to become his most famous work? Among his many compositions is a cantata, *In honour of the city of London*, a setting of William Dunbar's poem of 1500.

6 One of Britain's most important composers simulated the chimes of Big Ben in a symphony, which he called *A London Symphony*. Who is the composer and what is the number of the symphony?

## National Anthems

1 Who composed *La Marseillaise*?

2 Of which country is *La Brabançonne* the national anthem?

3 What is the English name for the Irish national anthem?

4 The authorship of which famous national anthem is wrongly attributed to John Bull and Henry Carey?

5 Who composed *The Emperor's Hymn*, the national anthem of Austria?

6 In which work did Tchaikovsky quote from the Czarist anthem *God preserve the Czar*?

## Italy

The titles of the six works listed below all have an Italian connection, but none of them was composed by an Italian. Can you name the composers?

1 *Italian Serenade* for string quartet, written in 1887.

2 *Capriccio Italien*, a symphonic poem, op. 45.

3 *Impressions d'Italie* an orchestral work written in 1887 and revised in 1913.

4 *Italienische Liederbuch* (*Italian song-book*) containing forty-six song settings, many of which were later orchestrated by the composer and by Max Reger.

5 *Harold in Italy*, a symphony with a solo viola part commissioned by Paganini, which is based on Byron's poem *Childe Harold's Pilgrimage*.

6 *Italian* Symphony, Symphony No. 4 in A major, op. 90, which was composed after a visit to Italy in 1833 but published only after the composer's death.

## We Love Paris

Each of the following composers has written music with the word 'Paris' in the title. Can you name the works?

1 Jacques Offenbach (1819–80).

2 George Gershwin (1898–1937).

3 Mozart (1719–87).

4 Offenbach (arranged by Manuel Rosenthal).

5 Johan Svendsen (1840–1911).

6 Frederick Delius (1862–1934).

# 6

# A Musical
# Detective Story

'And where were you on the night the crime was committed?' asked the detective.

'Well sir, being a music lover and something of an authority on music, on the evening in question I attended a concert at the Town Hall, a thing I do at least once a week.'

'I see,' replied the detective (being a bit of a music authority himself), 'and what was the programme that evening?'

The witness considered for a while and with apparent concentration said: 'The concert opened with the overture to *The Barber of Baghdad* by Rossini and was followed by a concerto. I heard a splendid performance by both soloist and orchestra of Bach's *Italian* Concerto. After the interval the first item was the incidental music by Tchaikovsky to *Swan White*, and the marvellous concert ended with César Franck's Symphony No. 1 in D minor. So, I'm sure you'll agree that I was so engrossed in all this music at the time the crime was committed, I couldn't possibly have done it.'

'Well, my son,' said the sleuth, 'I do believe I have you, because I'm afraid you've made no fewer than four mistakes in telling your tale, therefore I have no alternative but to ask you to accompany me to the nearest police station, where no doubt you will be put behind bars (musical ones of course!)'

What were the four mistakes the accused made which confirmed the detective's suspicion that he could not possibly have seen a programme, let alone heard the concert?

# 7

# Saints and Sinners

## Devilish Music

1 His devil had a 'trill'. Who was he and what was the work?
2 Who wrote a comic opera with the devil in the title?
3 Who wrote *The Devil in the Belfry*?
4 Liszt wrote four works with a devilish title. Can you name the works and their title?
5 Can you name the famous opera by Arrigo Boito that is based on a satanic character?
6 Who wrote *The Devil and Kate*?

## Saints and Sinners

1 Can you name three Passions by Bach that are based on the writings of saints?
2 Which oratorio by Mendelssohn tells the story of a saint?
3 Who wrote *Sins of my Old Age*?
4 Who wrote *The Seven Deadly Sins*?
5 Can you name two English composers who wrote works with the patron saint of music in the title, and what are the titles of the works?
6 Who wrote *Four Saints in Three Acts* to a text by Gertrude Stein?

# 8

# Gramophone Quiz

1 Who were the three pioneers of the modern gramophone record?
2 What is Caruso's earliest known recording?
3 What was the name of the first jazz orchestra ever recorded?
4 Who was 'Nıpper'?
5 What was 'Nipper' doing in the original painting?
6 What do Irving Kolodin, David Hall and Roland Gelatt have in common?
7 Who was Goddard Lieberson?
8 What is accepted as the official date of the birth of the gramophone and acoustic recording?
9 Who unveiled his invention on this date?
10 Of what were Edison's first cylinders made?
11 In what year did Émile Berliner unveil his invention and what was it?
12 Who is generally believed to be the first classical artist to be recorded for the gramophone record?
13 To whom did Berliner sell his gramophone rights and patents *outside* the United States in 1898?
14 When was electric recording first introduced.
15 In what year were the first records of Enrico Caruso made?
16 In 1909 the first orchestral records were released in England. Who was the conductor?
17 Which recording procedure was used before the advent of the electrical recording process?
18 When was the first long-playing record made and what was its speed?
19 When did the LP record make its commercial début in America?
20 When did the LP record make its commercial début in England and for which company?

21 When was the first stereophonic record released in the United Kingdom?

22 How many grooves does the average micro-groove LP record contain?

23 When was the first 'musicassette' as we know it today first introduced?

24 What is the rival system to the musicassette?

25 What is 'Dolby'?

26 What was Alan Dower Blumlein's contribution to the gramophone?

27 In 1924 HMV pressed the smallest playable gramophone record. What was it?

28 What is FFRR?

29 What is believed to be the oldest surviving recording?

30 Who, in 1907, laid the foundation stone of the HMV factory at Hayes, Middlesex?

31 Who was Charles Cros?

32 As what was the London branch of the American 'Victor' company known in its formative years?

33 What was the first classical LP to reach a sales figure of one million copies in the United States and the United Kingdom?

34 What was the first complete symphony ever recorded?

35 What were 'hill and dale' records?

36 What is digital recording?

37 Who were the first King and Queen of England to make a record?

38 Who, playing *Japanese Sandman* and *Whispering*, achieved the distinction of having the first million-seller record?

39 What is a 'Victrola'?

40 Who, in 1905, were the issuing companies of the first double-sided discs?

41 When was the first complete opera issued on gramophone records?

42 Can you name the three top awards given every year for outstanding gramophone records?

43 In what year was the magazine *Gramaphone* launched?

44 Who was the founder and first editor of *Gramophone*?

45  Who wrote the first complete string quartet to be put on record? Can you name it, and also say who played it?

46  When did Caruso make his last recording?

47  When did Toscanini make his first recording?

48  In the late nineteenth century Tennyson recited *The Charge of the Light Brigade* on to a cylinder. What was especially interesting about the 'background' music?

49  Name the Italian record label renowned for its vocal repertoire before 1910?

50  Who was Eldridge Johnson?

# 9
# Ballet, Opera and Operetta

## Ballet Music

1 Who composed the following ballets and what do they have in common? *The Nutcracker; Daphnis and Chloë; The Three-cornered Hat.*
2 Who composed *Prélude à l'Après-midi d'un faune* and *Scheherazade*, and what do the works have in common?
3 Can you name three composers who were at one time or another associated with Serge Diaghilev?
4 What is the usual title of the modern ballet that has as its subtitle *A game of chess between Love and Death*, and can you name the composer?
5 Can you name the ballet for which Charles Mackerras adapted the music from Gilbert and Sullivan operas?
6 What is the name of the ballet, the music of which was started by Léo Delibes and finished by Léon Minkus?

## Mr Gilbert and Mr Sullivan

1 Can you name the first opera resulting from Gilbert's collaboration with Sullivan?
2 What is the name of their last completed opera collaboration?
3 What is the first opera Sullivan set to music?
4 What is the name of the last opera on which Gilbert and Sullivan collaborated but which was in fact completed by Edward German?
5 By what title is *The King of Barataria* better known?
6 What is the alternative title for *Iolanthe*?

## Opera

1  What was Susanna's secret?
2  In which seventeenth-century composer's most famous opera do two of the main characters—Carolina (soprano) and Paolino (tenor)—share a secret, and can you name the opera and say what the secret is?
3  Who played poker for her lover's life?
4  What were Turandot's three riddles, which, if answered correctly, would win her hand in marriage, and can you supply the answers?
5  Who, in an opera by Wagner, had to find a 'guileless fool, totally ignorant of sin', in order to bring about the king's salvation?
6  When is opera said to have begun?

# 10

# Morning, Noon and Night

## The Four Elements

1 Mahler set six poems, translated from the Chinese, to music, scoring the work for two solo voices and orchestra. Can you name it?

2 Who composed the symphonic poem *Prometheus—The Poem of Fire?*

3 From which work does the 'Adoration of the Earth' come, and can you name the composer?

4 Can you give the titles of three works by Debussy that are associated with water?

5 Who used a wind machine in one of his last symphonies, and what is the name of the work?

6 What is the 'Fire' Symphony?

## Humour

1 Can you name the chamber work for string quartet and two french horns in which Mozart deliberately parodies incompetent musicians and composers?

2 Which work by a Hungarian composer begins with a gigantic 'sneeze' in the orchestra?

3 Can you name two composers who wrote piano works in a 'capricious' or 'fantastic' manner entitled *Humoresques* or *Humoreskes?*

4 What is the name of the ballet for which Vincenzo Tommasini (1878–1950) orchestrated a series of harpsichord sonatas by Domenico Scarlatti?

5 Who wrote an opera called *The Perfect Fool*, which was first produced at Covent Garden in 1923?
6 Which composer parodied himself in one of his best-known works, a composition for two pianos and orchestra? Can you name the work and say what is being parodied?

## Morning, Noon and Night

1 Who wrote the overture *Morning, Noon and Night in Vienna?*
2 Who wrote three symphonies entitled *Le Matin*, *Le Midi* and *Le Soir et la tempête?*
3 Can you name the composer who portrayed a faun during a particular time of day, and can you name the work and the famous dancer who choreographed and premièred the work as a ballet?
4 Who wrote the tone poem *Night ride and sunrise?*
5 A Norwegian composer's best-known work, the incidental music to an Ibsen play, has the time of day as the title of one of its movements. Can you name the composer, the complete work and the time of day?
6 Can you name two composers who wrote music inspired by Shakespeare's *A Midsummer Night's Dream?*

## Oh Death, Where is Thy Sting? (1)

1 Which English composer committed suicide in 1930, in Tite Street, Chelsea?
2 Which seventeenth-century composer stubbed his foot with a long baton while conducting and contracted gangrene from which he died?
3 Which twentieth-century composer died after developing blood poisoning from a bee sting?
4 Can you name the composer who died when his bicycle crashed into a wall?
5 Who was hit by the pole of a horse omnibus, which brought on an attack of pleurisy from which he never recovered?
6 Who died after falling off the rostrum following a brain haemorrhage?

## Oh Death, Where is Thy Sting? (2)

Can you identify the operas in which the following deaths occur?

1 The hero suffers from insane, unfounded jealousy and strangles the heroine in the final act, but, on being informed that she was innocent, he stabs himself, falling lifeless on her dead body.

2 Another jealous murder in a modern opera: the protagonist stabs to death his unfaithful mistress and then drowns himself in a muddy pool.

3 In this classic tear-jerker, the heroine dies of consumption after the hero has fought a duel and been forced to flee the country. He later returns to find the heroine on her death-bed.

4 The protagonist's love has been spurned for another; heartbroken he stabs the heroine to death and, in true operatic tradition, flings himself on the body as the curtain falls, crying 'I have killed her—may you arrest me. O——my adored——'.

5 Having kissed the severed head of a man whose execution she had requested, the heroine is herself ordered to be put to death by her step-father. She is crushed to death by the shields of the King's guard.

6 The hero in this opera meets his doom by being dragged down to Hell by the statue of someone he had previously killed in a duel after attempting to seduce his daughter.


## The Seasons

1 Can you name the woman composer who wrote a highly popular concert study called *Autumn?*

2 Who wrote *Spring Symphony*, op. 44, for soloists, chorus and orchestra?

3 Who wrote *The Winter Wind étude?*

4 Who wrote *A Summer Night on the River, In a Summer Garden, On hearing the first Cuckoo in Spring* and *A Song of Summer?*

5 Who wrote an oratorio called *The Seasons?*

6 Who wrote a series of concertos called *The Four Seasons?*

## Weddings

1 Who composed an opera in which a poor girl was bartered, and can you name this, his most popular work?
2 Whose wedding symphony was 'rustic'?
3 Whose wedding day was at Troldhaugen?
4 His Caprice for Piano and Strings is appropriate here because of the composer's alternative title. Can you name the composer and the alternative title?
5 Who composed the English opera *The Midsummer Marriage?*
6 Who wrote a *Wedding* Cantata?

# 11
# Lightning Quiz

How many questions can you answer correctly in the space of ten minutes?

1  Which composer was baptised Joannes Chrysostomus Wolfgangus Theophilus?

2  Where did the 'Village Romeo and Juliet' walk to?

3  Who was known as 'La Divina'?

4  Who is known as 'La Stupenda'?

5  Who wrote *Chopin* and *Paganini* for piano?

6  Which famous Austrian composer's life is the theme of the musical *Lilac Time*?

7  Which composer's life is the theme of the musical *Song of Norway*?

8  What is a 'chest' of viols?

9  What is a tromba marina?

10  Who composed the oratorio *Palestine*?

11  What do you know about *Lélio*?

12  What is known as the Boehm System?

13  Apart from Verdi, who else wrote an opera titled *Otello*?

14  Which composer died as a result of a bookcase falling on him?

15  In which opera by Mozart does he quote an aria from another of his operas?

16  Can you name the last three Masters of the King's/Queen's music?

17  Can you name two operas composed by Karl Goldmark?

18  Who composed the opera *Oberto, Conte di San Bonifacio*, and what is its significance?

19  Which composer was also a distinguished opera librettist?

20  What is the special link between the opera *Intermezzo* and its composer?

# 12

# The Old Curiosity Shop

### The Old Curiosity Shop (1)

1 What is a clavicytherium?
2 Can you name a rare keyboard instrument that combines an organ and harpsichord?
3 Which Victorian instrument was described in an advertisement as containing 236 broad steel tongues, 14 harmonium reeds, a triangle and a drum?
4 If you are lucky you might come across in a second-hand music shop a set of twenty little piano pieces all on large scale sheets and enclosed in an artist's portfolio complete with tapes to tie it with. Do you know what this music is?
5 An instrument, which is called the hurdy-gurdy in English, has been revived but originals are occasionally to be found in antique shops. Can you describe it?
6 Shops selling old prints and drawings occasionally have a drawing by an English composer who played *God save great George our King* on the organ when he was only two-and-a-half years old. At the age of four he was giving daily organ recitals in London. Who was he?

### The Old Curiosity Shop (2)

1 What is a 'Jingling Johnny'?
2 Can you name two works by Ralph Vaughan Williams for unlikely musical instruments?
3 Which German king was also a composer?
4 What is a sarrusophone?
5 Which well-known composer was also a butcher's boy?
6 Can you name an English composer who was also a painter, an author and a member of the diplomatic service?

## The Old Spuriosity Shop

Can you name the correct composers of the following works, which are often wrongly attributed?

1 Weber's *Last Waltz*.
2 Bach's *Bist du bei mir* from the Anna Magdalena Book.
3 Arne's *The Lass with the delicate air*.
4 Haydn's *Toy* Symphony.
5 Martini's *Plaisir d'amour*.
6 Beethoven's *Jena* Symphony.

# 13

# Miscellaneous

## A-hunting We Will Go

1 Who wrote *The King's Hunt*?
2 Who composed a symphonic poem in which the huntsman was warned not to go hunting on the Sabbath; but he did, with disastrous results?
3 Probably one of the most famous hunting scenes in music is an interlude for orchestra and chorus from a mammoth opera by Berlioz. Do you know what the scene is called and from which opera it comes?
4 Who set to music *The Royal Hunt of the Sun*?
5 Can you identify a symphony and a quartet by Haydn that are both nicknamed *La Chasse*?
6 Can you name a string quartet by Mozart that carries the title *The Hunt*, and say why it is so called?

## Abbreviations

What do the following abbreviations mean?
1 A.R.A.M.; A.R.C.M.; A.R.C.O.
2 L.P.O.; S.N.O.; R.L.P.O.
3 Mus.B. (or B.Mus.); Mus.D. (or D.Mus.); G.S.M.
4 Ob.; Obb.; Op.
5 G.R.N.C.M.; A.S.C.A.P.; M.C.P.S.
6 E.M.I.; S.P.N.M.; I.S.M.

## Alternative Titles

All the following musical works are better known by their usual titles. Can you identify them?
1 A ballet by Delibes subtitled *The Girl with the Enamel Eyes*.

2 An opera by Rossini subtitled *The Triumph of Goodness*.
3 An opera by Mozart subtitled *The School for Lovers*.
4 An opera, first performed in Vienna in 1805, with the subtitle *Wedded Love*.
5 A well-known ballet by Ferdinand Hérold subtitled *Vain Precautions*.
6 A piano work by Schumann subtitled *Dainty Scenes on Four Notes*.

## Baroque

1 When was the Baroque period?
2 Can you name the court composer who was Lully's greatest successor and who was especially famous for his numerous brilliant keyboard compositions?
3 What is the origin of the word 'baroque'?
4 What is the prevailing international baroque standard pitch?
5 Can you name the style of voice production that was perfected in the Baroque period?
6 How many so-called sonatas did Domenico Scarlatti write?

## Battle Music

1 Can you name a rather simple work for piano by the Czech composer Franz Kotzwara, who, in 1791, committed suicide in a house of ill repute in London?
2 Do you know the name of an opera from Verdi's middle period about the wars of the Lombard League which is seldom revived today?
3 Which symphonic poem by Liszt, composed in 1857, was inspired by a fresco of Kaulbach?
4 Prokofiev composed some music for a film by Eisenstein that he later developed into a cantata. The thrilling fifth section bears the name of a battle. What is the work, and what is the title of the battle movement?
5 Which four-act opera by Rimsky-Korsakov, which was first performed in 1907, contains a battle scene, and can you name that scene?

6 Beethoven was originally asked to write this work for the Panharmonicon, a mechanical instrument invented by Johann
Nepomuk Mälzel, but he also scored it for orchestra at the
same time, the idea being that both versions would go on
concert tours. It was one of his greatest successes at the time,
although the work is out of favour today. It is in two parts,
'The Battle' and 'The Victory Symphony'. Do you know the
complete title of the work?

### Christmas Music

1 Who composed the *Christmas Oratorio*?
2 Who composed *Christmas* Concertos (two composers)?
3 Who composed the *Carol* Symphony?
4 Who composed *A Ceremony of Carols*?
5 Who composed *A Christmas Cantata* for chorus and
orchestra?
6 Who composed *Hodie* (*This Day*), Christmas Cantata, in
1953–4?

### Dedicated to You

1 Which well-known orchestral work by a famous British composer is 'Dedicated to my friends pictured within'?
2 Which work by Beethoven was for 'Elise'?
3 To whom was Mendelssohn's Symphony No. 3 in A, op. 56,
the *Scottish*, dedicated?
4 Whose well-known Violin Concerto in D, op. 77, was dedicated to Joseph Joachim, the famous violinist, composer and
conductor?
5 To whom was Bach's *Musical Offering* (*Das Musikalischer
Opfer*) offered?
6 To whom is Ravel's only quartet, in F major, written in 1902,
dedicated?

### Innovators

1 Can you name the first collection of music for virginals to be
*published* in England?

2 Who composed what were, in all probability, the first *published* sonatas for the piano?

3 Which composer introduced the typewriter as an orchestral instrument?

4 Who inaugurated the first concerts open to the general public 'for a payment at the door'?

5 Can you name the family that, more than any other, can be credited with the modern revival of early stringed, wind and keyboard instruments?

6 Who invented a system of mixed notation that did away with the conventional staves and notes, and was based on the old syllabic system—do (ut), re, mi, etc—and can you name the system?

## Instruments of the Orchestra

1 Can you name the instruments usually found in the woodwind section of the orchestra?

2 Which instruments are usually found in the brass section of the orchestra?

3 Can you name at least eight instruments found in the percussion section of the orchestra?

4 How many strings does the harp usually have?

5 On which instruments are nut, scroll and ribs to be found?

6 From which instrument does the orchestra take its pitch for tuning and for which note?

## Invitation to the Dance

The correct answers have an association with a ball or dance.

1 Can you name a three-act opera by Verdi in which the main characters are Riccardo (tenor), Amelia (soprano), Renato (baritone), Oscar (soprano) and Ulrica (mezzo soprano)?

2 Which ballet by Geoffrey Toye ranks as his most popular composition?

3 Can you name a highly entertaining and sophisticated ballet, choreographed by Benois and with music by Johann Strauss arranged and orchestrated by Antal Dorati, which involves a

group of young cadets visiting a girls' school for their graduation ceremonies?

4 Which one-act opera buffa, composed by Gian-Carlo Menotti (b. 1911) and first performed in 1937, was the first American comic opera to be staged at the Metropolitan Opera House, New York?

5 Can you name a work by Weber, his op. 65 (1819), which he called a 'rondeau brillant'? It incorporates a slow introduction and a waltz in the middle section, and it ends with an epilogue. It was brilliantly orchestrated by Berlioz in 1841, and later by the great Austrian conductor/composer Felix Weingartner. It was taken up by Diaghilev's Ballets Russes and is still successfully performed as *Le Spectre de la Rose*.

6 Which concert overture was written by Arthur Sullivan (1842–1900) in 1870?

## The King of Instruments

1 He was born in Alsace, became a medical student and an organ pupil of Widor in Paris, but spent much of his time in Africa. He was an authority on the music of one composer in particular. Who was he, and who was the composer?

2 Which composer, more generally associated with the theatre than the organ-loft, succeeded César Franck in 1890 as organist of the fashionable Paris church of Sainte-Clotilde?

3 Organ building tends to go in families. Can you name one celebrated family from England, from France and from Germany?

4 Which organist, born in Westcliff-on-Sea, studied at the Royal Academy of Music before emigrating to the United States where he made his name as a recording artist?

5 An organ piece by an English organist and composer, who died in Los Angeles, was turned into a very popular song. Who was the composer, what was the original title, and what was the name of the song?

6 Why is Bach's Chorale Prelude *Wir glauben all* from Part 3 of the *Clavierübung* known as the 'Giant Fugue'?

## Monarchs

1 Who wrote an opera called *Henry VIII*?
2 Who composed the *Henry VIII* dances?
3 Where does the *Queen Mab* Scherzo come from and who composed it?
4 Who composed the *King Christian II* Suite, op. 27?
5 Who composed the opera *The Queen of Spades*?
6 Who composed *The Three Elizabeths* Suite?

## The Numbers Game

1 How many operas are there in Wagner's *Der Ring des Nibelungen* cycle?
2 What is known as the *Symphony of a Thousand*?
3 How many operas did Gilbert and Sullivan write and how many can you name?
4 How many children did Johann Sebastian Bach father, and of the survivors who became composers or musicians?
5 How many notes does a concert grand piano have?
6 How many string quartets, piano sonatas, symphonies and concertos did Beethoven write. Can you name their opus numbers and keys in these categories?

## The Odd One Out

Can you identify the odd one out in each of these six questions, and can you say why?
1 Verdi; Puccini; Donizetti; Bellini.
2 *King Priam*; *King Stephen*; *King Roger*.
3 *La Mer*; *The Water Music*; *Sea Pictures*.
4 No. 37, K. 444; No. 38, K. 504; No. 39, K. 543.
5 *St Paul*; *St Nicholas*; *St Ludmilla*.
6 Zabaleta; Robles; Domingo.

## The Pioneers

1 Who was the 'creator of the Viennese waltz'?
2 Who was the 'creator of French Opéra Comique'?
3 Who was the 'father of the French operetta'?

4  Who was the 'father of modern orchestration'?
5  Who was the first German piano maker?
6  Who was the 'father of the waltz'?

## Variations on a Theme

Can you name the original themes used in the following variations?
1  Variations on a theme by Paganini, op. 35 for piano by Brahms.
2  Variations and Fugue on a theme by Handel, op. 24 for piano by Brahms.
3  *Young Person's Guide to the Orchestra*, op. 34 (Variations and Fugue on a theme of Purcell) by Benjamin Britten.
4  Totentanz, G. 126 for piano and orchestra by Liszt; Rhapsody on a theme of Paganini for piano and orchestra by Rachmaninov; *Symphonie fantastique*, op. 14 by Berlioz.
5  Variations on a nursery song, op. 25 for piano and orchestra by Ernö Dohnanyi.
6  Variations for piano and orchestra, op. 2 by Chopin.

## Musical Terms

Here are six pairs of musical directions—can you tell the difference between each pair?
1  *Andante* and *allegro*.
2  *Lento* and *presto*.
3  *Diminuendo* and *crescendo*.
4  *Pianissimo* and *fortissimo*.
5  *Accelerando* and *rallentando*.
6  *Scherzando* and *tremolando*.

# 14
# Who and What?

## What is the Difference?

1 Can you distinguish between Puccini and Piccini?
2 Can you name four composers with the surname Strauss and belonging to the same family?
3 What is the difference between clarino and clarina?
4 Can you name three composers who wrote a *Pastoral* symphony?
5 What is the difference between attacca and attacco?
6 There are two quite different works with the title *Calm Sea and Prosperous Voyage*. Who wrote them?

## What is the Question?

Here are the answers to six fairly simple musical questions. Can you suggest appropriate questions?
1 A composition for orchestra, generally in the form of a sonata, consisting of several movements, but usually with fuller development and greater breadth of treatment.
2 He was a scientist, musician and the author of the 'Systematic, chronological and complete Catalogue of Mozart's works', published in 1862.
3 It is the distance from one note to the next nearest one (either way), of the same letter name—i.e., middle C to the next C, above or below.
4 No. 31 in D, K. 297; No. 35 in D, K. 385; No. 36 in C, K. 425; No. 38 in D, K. 504; No. 41 in C, K. 551.
5 Dorian, Phrygian, Lydian, Mixolydian, Aeolian and Ionian.
6 *Farewell*, *Maria Theresa*, *Oxford*, *Surprise* and *Drum roll*.

## Who Am I?

1 He was born in Bilbao in 1806, composed three string quartets, a symphony and many other works before dying of consumption in Paris at the age of nineteen.

2 Born in Munich, 1864, he began composing at the age of six and by the age of twenty had composed a number of pieces on classical models. He became influenced by Brahms although he finally adopted the Berlioz, Liszt and Wagner style of orchestral programme music. Best known for his operas, symphonic works and songs, he died in 1949.

3 Born in Genoa in 1782 the son of a poor shopkeeper, he appeared publicly at the age of eleven, ran away in his late teens and started concert touring on his own account. The most wonderful and original of violin players, his technique was marvellous and, together with his personal eccentricities, his 'tricks of virtuosity' and his 'dazzling genius', made him the wonder of his age. His remarkable performances on a single string have probably never been equalled.

4 Born in Prague in 1794 the son of a Jewish merchant, he played a piano concerto of his own composition in public at the age of fourteen. He went to Vienna shortly afterwards and while there prepared the pianoforte score for Beethoven's *Fidelio* under the composer's supervision. After continental tours, he lived mostly in London from 1841 until 1846 as a teacher and composer, writing eight piano concertos, a grand septet and other chamber music. One of his pupils was Mendelssohn. He died in Leipzig in 1870.

5 Born at Raiding, Hungary, in 1811, he started to learn the piano at the age of six and played in public at the age of nine. He studied the piano under Czerny and theory under Salieri, the former teacher of Schubert, in Vienna in 1821 and 1822. Renowned for his feats of piano technique, poetic feeling and expression, his piano playing attracted the attention and admiration of Beethoven, and Pope Pius IX conferred on him the title of 'Abbé'. He composed concertos, symphonic poems, rhapsodies, fantasias, *études*, paraphrases and transcriptions, and songs. He died at Bayreuth in 1886.

6 Born in Leipzig in 1819, she was trained by her father Friedrich Wieck from her fifth year, giving her first public programme in 1828. She married a famous composer in 1840, and
became an authoritative interpreter of his work, doing much
to make them famous.

## Who Said? (1)

To which composers are the following quotations attributed?

1 'Beethoven can write music, thank God, but he can do
nothing else on earth.'

2 'To us musicians the work of Beethoven parallels the pillars of
smoke and fire which led the Israelites through the desert, a
pillar of smoke to lead us by day, and a pillar of fire to light the
night, so that we may march ahead both day and night. His
darkness and his light equally trace for us the road we must
follow; both the one and the other are a perpetual com-
mandment, an infallible revelation.'

3 'Oh Mozart, immortal Mozart, what countless images of a
brighter and better world thou hast stamped upon our souls!'

4 'I would like to thank Beethoven, Brahms, Wagner, Strauss,
Rimsky-Korsakov . . .'

5 'Poor Devils! Where do they come from? At what age are they
sent to the slaughter house? What is done with their bones?
Where do such animals pasture in the daytime? Do they have
females and young? How many of them handled the brush
before being reduced to the broom?'

6 'I like to play Bach because it is interesting to play a good
fugue; but I do not regard him, in common with many others,
as a great genius. Handel is only fourth-rate, he is not even interesting. I sympathise with Gluck in spite of his poor creative
gift. I also like some things of Haydn. These four great
masters have been surpassed by Mozart. They are rays which
are extinguished by Mozart's sun.'

## Who Said (2)

1 Who wrote the poem that opens 'What is life but a series of preludes to that unknown song whose first solemn note is sounded by death?' and that inspired Liszt's symphonic poem *Les Préludes*?

2 Who said: 'There is no shadow of death anywhere in Mozart's music. Even his own funeral was a failure. It was dispersed by a shower of rain; and to this day nobody knows where he was buried or whether he was buried at all or not. Depend on it, they had no sooner put up their umbrellas and bolted for the nearest shelter than he got up, shook off his bones into the common grave of the people, and soared off into universality.'

3 Who said of music: 'It is the only sensual pleasure without vice.'

4 Whose famous testament includes the following quotation, and under what circumstances was it written? 'But what a humiliation, when any one standing beside me could hear at a distance a flute that I cannot hear, or any one heard the shepherd singing, and I could not distinguish a sound! Such circumstances brought me to the brink of despair, and well-nigh made me put an end to my life: nothing but my art held my hand. Ah! it seemed to me impossible to quit the world before I produced all that I felt myself called to accomplish.'

5 Do you know who recorded this message on a phonograph for Thomas Alva Edison? 'Dear Mr Edison, for myself, I can only say that I am astonished and somewhat terrified at the result of this evening's experiment. Astonished at the wonderful form you have developed and terrified at the thought that so much hideous and bad music will be put on records forever.'

6 Who said 'The sound of a harpsichord: two skeletons copulating on a galvanised tin roof'?

# Answers

# 1 ANIMAL, VEGETABLE AND MINERAL

## Animals

1 Frédéric Chopin (1810–49): Waltz, op. 34 no. 3; Domenico Scarlatti (1685–1757): Sonata K. 30 for harpsichord. The title of the first concerns the story (probably apocryphal) that Chopin's cat jumped on to the keyboard of his piano as he was in the midst of composition, and the notes struck by its paws as it walked suggested to the composer the *appoggiatura* passage for section four of the waltz. A similar story is told concerning Scarlatti's *Cat's Fugue*.

2 Waltz in D flat, op. 64 no. 1. This is the most popular of all Chopin's waltzes, and the rather fanciful story attached to it is that George Sand's dog was running round and round chasing its own tail in the presence of the composer, who immediately sat down and improvised the waltz.

3 Symphony No. 82 in C. This symphony probably gained its nickname from the theme of the finale, which has a bagpipe-like sound suggesting music for a performing bear.

4 *The Cunning Little Vixen* (first performed 1924).

5 *Mazeppa*, G. 138, from *Grandes études pour le piano* (1838). This was also included as the fourth of the *Études d'exécution transcendante* for piano (1851); the orchestral tone poem was completed in 1857.

6 Although there are fourteen sections in the work, only eight kinds of animal are mentioned by name. The movements in full are: 1. 'Introduction and Royal March of the Lion'; 2. 'Cocks and Hens'; 3. 'Wild Asses'; 4. 'Tortoises'; 5. 'Elephants'; 6. 'Kangaroos' 7. 'Aquarium'; 8. 'People with Long Ears'; 9. 'Cuckoo in the Woods'; 10. 'Aviary'; 11. 'Pianists'; 12. 'Fossils'; 13. 'The Swan'; 14. 'Finale'.

## Birds

1 Joseph Haydn (1732–1809): Symphony No. 83 in G minor. In the first movement, Allegro spiritoso, the second subject was thought by the Parisians to sound like the clucking of hens.

2 *The Golden Cockerel* (first performed 1909), by Nicolai Rimsky-Korsakov (1844–1908).

3 This is 'The Swan', from *Carnival of Animals* by Camille Saint-Saëns. Nash's verse refers, of course, to Anna Pavlova, the legendary ballerina, most famous for her performance of the 'Dying Swan' solo danced to Saint-Saëns' music.

4 A movement from *Pictures from an Exhibition* by Modeste Mussorgsky (1839–81).

5 *The Two Pigeons* (first performed 5 March 1886).

6 *The Pines of Rome* by Ottorino Respighi (1879–1936).

## Children

1 Bizet: *Jeux d'enfants* (*Children's Games*), composed for piano duet (four hands at one piano); four of the twelve movements were later orchestrated by the composer. Debussy: *Children's Corner* for piano, consisting of the following movements: 'Doctor Gradus ad Parnassum', 'Jimbo's Lullaby', 'Doll's Serenade', 'The Snow is Dancing', 'Little Shepherd' and 'Golliwog's Cake-walk'. Schumann: *Scenes from Childhood* (or, to give it its German title, *Kinderscenen*), op. 15, which consists of thirteen piano pieces.

2 Maurice Ravel (1875–1937). This one-act opera or *fantaisie lyrique* has a libretto by the popular novelist Colette and was first performed in Monte Carlo in 1925.

3 *Hansel and Gretel* by Engelbert Humperdinck, an opera in three acts derived from the fairy tale by the Brothers Grimm (first performed 1893).

4 Sir Edward Elgar (1857–1934). He first composed the *Wand of Youth* music at the age of twelve, as incidental music to a children's play. Later he rewrote it and arranged it as two orchestral suites (op. 1a and op. 1b). The *Nursery Suite* was dedi-

cated to the Duchess of York (the present Queen Mother) and her two daughters Princess Elizabeth and Princess Margaret Rose.

5 Roger Quilter (1877–1953). It was based on tunes from Walter Crane's book of nursery rhymes.

6 Sir Michael Tippett, in 1940. It has a text that combines religious themes with contemporary problems, and makes use of negro spirituals.

## Colours

1 *A Colour Symphony*, written in 1922 and revised in 1932, by Sir Arthur Bliss (1891–1975).

2 Daniel Auber (1782–1871). His opera in three acts, *Le Domino noir*, with libretto by Scribe, was first performed at the Paris Opéra Comique on 2 December 1837.

3 Reinhold Glière (1875–1956).

4 Claude Debussy, in 1915.

5 *On the Beautiful Blue Danube*, by Johann Strauss the younger.

6 Virgil Thomson (b. 1896).

## Doctors of Music

1 Claude Debussy. This is the first piece in his *Children's Corner* suite, written in 1908. The title is a humorous reference to Muzio Clementi's collection of piano studies, *Gradus ad Parnassum*, which numbers 100 instructive and progressive pieces.

2 Léo Delibes. The work is the ballet *Coppélia* (1870); the doctor here is a toymaker who has made a remarkably lifelike doll—Coppélia herself.

3 Georges Bizet. *Doctor Miracle* is a one-act operetta, which in 1856 won for its composer a prize offered by Jacques Offenbach for a short opera with this title. A joint winner was one of Bizet's fellow students, Alexandre Lecocq. The character Doctor Miracle also appears in the third episode of Offenbach's own *Tales of Hoffmann*.

4 Ferruccio Busoni (1866–1924). His opera of this title was completed after his death by his pupil Philipp Jarnach (b. 1892). There are a number of works based on the Faust legend, including operas by Charles Gounod, Louis Spohr and Zölner, and *A Faust Symphony* by Franz Liszt.
5 Jacques Offenbach. This is the title of an operetta in three acts, first produced in 1877.
6 Johann Strauss the younger. Doctor Falke is a leading character in the delightful operetta *Die Fledermaus* (*The Bat*).

## Fishy Stories

1 Franz Schubert (1797–1828). The song is *Die Forelle* (*The Trout*), D. 550, and the Quintet for piano and strings in A, D. 667, is also known as the 'Trout' Quintet because it includes a set of variations on the song in the fourth movement.
2 'Poissons d'or' ('Goldfish').
3 Alan Hovhaness, an American composer born in 1911.
4 Alan Rawsthorne (1905–71).
5 Ireland. The heroine, 'sweet Molly Malone', sold her wares in the streets of Dublin—which she was later to haunt.
6 . . . *Herring*. First produced at Glyndebourne in 1947.

## Flowers

1 *Daisies*, op. 38 no. 3, and *Lilacs*, op. 21 no. 5.
2 *Das Veilchen* (*The Violet*), K. 476.
3 *Heidenröslein* (*Wayside Rose*), D. 257, a setting of the poem by Goethe.
4 *Der Rosenkavalier*, by Richard Strauss. The rose is presented to Sophie by Count Octavian on behalf of another man to whom she is betrothed, but Octavian and Sophie fall in love at first sight.
5 Jean Sibelius: his op. 36 no. 1.
6 On certain stringed and keyboard instruments. The sound holes in lutes, guitars, virginals and harpsichords are generally known as roses.

## Fruit

1 Erik Satie (1866–1925). They form a composition for piano duet.
2 *The Love for Three Oranges*, by Serge Prokofiev (1891–1953). This satirical comedy was first produced in Leningrad in 1921.
3 Peter Ilich Tchaikovsky (1840–93). The piece referred to is, of course, 'The Dance of the Sugar-Plum Fairy', from his ballet *The Nutcracker*.
4 A character in George Gershwin's opera *Porgy and Bess*.
5 Morton Subotnick (b. 1933).
6 Ludwig van Beethoven. His only oratorio, it was first performed in 1803.

## Gardens

2 *The Garden of Fand*. Although not Irish by descent, Bax was greatly influenced in his early compositions by the poems of W. B. Yeats and the folk music of Ireland. The *Garden of Fand* was his last 'Celtic' orchestral work.
2 *In a Summer Garden*.
3 *In a Monastery Garden,* by Albert Ketèlbey.
4 'Jardins sous la pluie' ('Gardens in the Rain').
5 Mary Garden.
6 *Country Gardens*, by Percy Grainger (British Folk Music Settings, no. 22).

## Golden Music

1 *The Golden Age* and *The Golden Key*.
2 *The Golden Legend*.
3 It is an aria from Act 1, scene 2 of Gounod's *Faust*, sung by Méphistophélès (bass).
4 Henry Purcell. It is the ninth sonata in F major from his Ten Sonatas of Four Parts for two violins, cello and continuo.
5 *Das Rheingold* (*The Rhine Gold*), from *Der Ring des Nibelungen* (*The Ring of the Nibelung*), by Richard Wagner. It is the first opera in the cycle.
6 *The Golden Cockerel* (*Le Coq d'Or*).

## Here Come the Boys

1 Pietro Mascagni (1863–1945). First produced October 1891.

2 Arrigo Boito (1842–1918), composer and librettist. First performed May 1924.

3 Giacomo Puccini (1858–1924). First produced April 1889. This four-act work was Puccini's least successful opera. (It was his second opera.)

4 Richard Wagner (1813–83). This is the third in the tetralogy comprising *Das Rheingold* (*The Rhine Gold*), *Die Walküre* (*The Valkyrie*), *Siegfried* and *Götterdämmerung* (*Twilight of the Gods*), first performed as a cycle in Bayreuth, August 1876.

5 George Frideric Handel (1685–1759). The composer's first London opera, it was first produced in February 1711, with great success.

6 Carl Maria von Weber (1786–1826). The work, also known as *The Elf King's Oath*, was commissioned for Covent Garden and first performed there, with the composer conducting, in 1826. It has no connection with Shakespeare's *A Midsummer Night's Dream*, which was turned into an opera in 1960 by Benjamin Britten. There is also an opera called *Oberon, King of the Fairies* by Anton Wranitzky (1761–1820), but it is seldom performed today.

## Here Come the Girls

1 Alban Berg (1885–1935). The composer left the third and final act unfinished, but it has since been completed by Freidrich Cerha, who has won universal acclaim for his work. The opera had its first performance in the completed form in Paris on 24 February 1979.

2 Friedrich von Flotow (1812–83). The work is also known as *Der Markt von Richmond* (*Richmond Market*).

3 Vincenzo Bellini (1801–35). This is his most famous opera.

4 Richard Strauss (1864–1949). The work was first performed in Dresden in 1933.

5 Richard Strauss. This is one of the few operas by Strauss on which Hugo von Hofmannsthal did not collaborate.

6  Pietro Mascagni (1863–1945). The opera was first produced in 1898.

## I'll Drink to That

1  *La Traviata*. First performed in Venice, 1853.
2  *The Merry Wives of Windsor*, by Otto Nicolai (1810–49). First produced in Berlin, 1849.
3  *Otello*. The instigator of the quaffing is that devious character Iago. (Incidentally *Otello* has been described as the 'perfect' opera.)
4  *Cavalleria Rusticana*, by Pietro Mascagni (1863–1945). First produced in Rome, May 1890.
5  'Il segreto per essere felice' ('O the secret of bliss in perfection'), sung by Maffio Orsini (contralto). The aria was a showpiece of the great contralto Ernestine Schumann-Heink (1861–1936).
6  *Die Fledermaus*, by Johann Strauss the younger. First performed in Vienna, April 1874.

## In the Countryside

1  Beethoven's Symphony No. 6 in F, op. 68, *Pastoral*.
2  *From Bohemia's Woods and Fields*.
3  *Pastoral* Symphony.
4  *Pastoral*.
5  'Waldweben' ('Forest Murmurs').
6  *Pastorale d'été* (*Summer Pastoral*).

## Musical Jewels

1  'Ah je ris' (Jewel Song), sung by Marguérite.
2  *Gioielle della madonna* (*The Jewels of the Madonna*).
3  *Les diamants de la couronne* (*The Crown Diamonds*).
4  *Les pêcheurs de perles* (*The Pearl Fishers*).
5  *The Emerald Isle*. First produced in London, 1901.
6  *Jewels*.

# 2 MUSICIANS

## Composer Last

1 Albert Roussel (1869–1937) *or* Nicolai Rimsky-Korsakov (1844–1908).
2 Alexander Borodin (1833–87).
3 Modeste Mussorgsky (1839–81).
4 Hector Berlioz (1803–69).
5 Alan Rawsthorne (1905–71).
6 Emmanuel Chabrier (1841–94). Other notable law students are Handel, Tchaikovsky, Arne, Schumann and Sibelius.

## Composers

1 Felix Mendelssohn (full name Jacob Ludwig Felix Mendelssohn-Bartholdy): *Elijah*. The popular orchestral composition of the seventeen-year-old Mendelssohn is, of course, the overture to *A Midsummer Night's Dream*.
2 Jean-Baptiste Lully (or Lulli).
3 Henry Purcell.
4 Zoltán; Dietrich; Nicholas.
5 Johann Sebastian Bach (1685–1750); Frédéric Chopin (1810–49); George Frideric Handel (1685–1759).
6 Hugo Wolf (1860–1903): *Der Corregidor* (*The Magistrate*), composed in 1895 and produced in Mannheim in 1896.

## Composers on the Screen (1)

1 Nicolai Rimsky-Korsakov (1844–1908).
2 Richard Wagner (1813–83).
3 Ludwig van Beethoven (1770–1827).
4 Franz Schubert (1797–1828).
5 Johann Strauss the younger (1825–99).
6 Peter Ilich Tchaikovsky (1840–93).

## Composers on the Screen (2)

1 *Symphonie Fantastique*.
2 *Mahler*.
3 *Song of Norway*.
4 *Mr Gilbert and Mr Sullivan*.
5 *Song of Love*.
6 *Song of Love*.

## Cellists

1 Pablo (Pau) Casals.
2 Mstislav Rostropovich and Galina Vishnevskaya.
3 Guilhermina Suggia.
4 Beatrice Harrison.
5 Alfredo Carlo Piatti.
6 Pierre Fournier.

## Conductors

1 Leopold Stokowski. The films were *The Big Broadcast of 1927*, *One Hundred Men and a Girl* and *Fantasia*—a collaboration with Walt Disney.
2 Sir Charles Hallé.
3 Sir Thomas Beecham.
4 Bruno Walter (real name, Bruno Walter Schlesinger).
5 Arturo Toscanini.
6 Wilhelm Furtwängler.

## Pianists

1 Vladimir de Pachman.
2 Ignacy (Jan) Paderewski.
3 Alfred Cortot.
4 Franz Liszt.
5 Benno Moiseiwitsch.
6 Vladimir Horowitz.

## Singers

1 Dame Nellie Melba.
2 Enrico Caruso.
3 Mattia Battistini.
4 Fyodor Shalyapin (Chaliapin).
5 Kathleen Ferrier.
6 Maria Callas.

## Violinists

1 Jascha Heifetz.
2 Niccolò Paganini.
3 Fritz Kreisler.
4 Yehudi Menuhin.
5 Joseph Joachim.
6 David Oistrakh and his son Igor.

## Wagner

1 *Tannhäuser*; *The Flying Dutchman*; *Tristan and Isolde*.
2 *Lohengrin*; *Tannhäuser*; *Die Meistersinger von Nürnberg*.
3 The house is situated at Triebschen near Lucerne; the people of the city of Lucerne and the Swiss Friends of Bayreuth rescued it and turned it into the Wagner Museum in 1933. It now houses an outstanding collection of Wagner's manuscripts, scenery sketches, verses and letters.
4 *Die Hochzeit*. This opera of 1832 was never finished, while the other two, composed in 1833–4 and 1835–6 respectively, were the first Wagner operas to be produced on stage.
5 Symphony No. 9 in D minor, *Choral*.
6 There are eight in all: Overture in B flat major, *Drumbeat* (1830); Overture in C major (1830); Concert Overture in D minor (1831); Overture to Raupach's *König Enzio* (1832); Overture to T. Apel's *Christoph Columbus* (1835); *Polonia* Overture (1836); *Rule, Britannia* Overture (1837); Overture to Goethe's *Faust* (1855), which Wagner had originally intended as the first movement of a *Faust* symphony in 1840, but later revised as an overture.

## With a Little Help from my Friends

1 Composed for the piano and subsequently orchestrated by Hector Berlioz. There is a second, less well-known orchestral arrangement by Felix Weingartner (1863–1942).

2 Originally composed for organ and scored by a number of different composers. The versions most frequently played are those by 'Klenovsky' (Sir Henry Wood) and Leopold Stokowski.

3 Originally for piano and again orchestrated by a number of musicians. The most familiar arrangement is that by Maurice Ravel.

4 Composed by Fauré but orchestrated by Charles Koechlin (1867–1951).

5 Composed for piano (four hands); orchestrated by Henri Büsser (1872–1973).

6 Orchestrated by Arnold Schönberg (1874–1951).

## Women Composers

1 Elisabeth Lutyens (b. 1906), daughter of Sir Edwin Lutyens and widow of Edward Clark. Ballet: *Birthday of the Infanta*.

2 Lili Boulanger (1893–1918), sister of Nadia. Cantata: *Fanor et Hélène* (for which she won the Prix de Rome).

3 Dame Ethel Smyth (1858–1944). Opera: *The Wreckers*.

4 Germaine Tailleferre (b. 1892), the only woman member of 'Les Six'. (The others were Georges Auric, Louis Durey, Arthur Honegger, Darius Milhaud and Francis Poulenc.) Harp Concertino.

5 Marie Szymanowska (1795–1831). A lot of short piano pieces, and two songs—charming but of no great importance. Her best work is in her twenty-four mazurkas for piano. Her compatriot was Karol Szymanowski (1882–1937).

6 Mrs H. H. A. Beach (1867–1944). (This is how she always styled herself, though her full name was Amy Marcy Beach.) *Gaelic Symphony*, piano pieces, Mass, etc.

# 3 QUICK GENERAL MUSICAL KNOWLEDGE QUIZ

1  Symphony No. 3 in E flat, op. 55, *Eroica*. However, Beethoven later tore up the dedication when Napoleon crowned himself Emperor.

2  104 (The generally accepted number).

3  The odd man out is Henri Wieniawski (1835–80). He was a famous violinist and composer, while the others—Jan Paderewski (1860–1941), Theodor Leschetizky (1830–1915) and Leopold Godowsky (1870–1938)—were all famous pianists.

4  Richard Addinsell (b. 1904), John Addison (b. 1920), John Adson (d. *c*1640), Walter Alcock (1864–1947), Richard Alison, Allison or Alyson (*fl* seventeenth century), William Alwyn (b. 1905), Thomas Arne (1710–78), Richard Arnell (b. 1917), Malcolm Arnold (b. 1921), Thomas Attwood (1765–1838), Charles Avison (1709–70).

5  Friedrich Zachow or Zachau (1663–1712), Jan Zacz (1699–1773), Riccardo Zandonai (1883–1944), Adone Zecchi (b. 1904), Johann Zelenka (1679–1745), Carl Zelter (1758–1832), Zesso (*c*1500), Marc' Antonio Ziani (1633–1715), Karl Ziehrer (1843–1922), Efrem Zimbalist (b. 1889), Bernd Zimmermann (1918–70), Nicola Zingarelli (1752–1837), Domenico Zipoli (1688–1726).

6  Licentiate of Trinity College, London; Licentiate of the Guildhall School of Music.

7  Schumann. The variations are so called because they were dedicated to Countess Abegg and consist of themes made up from the notes A, B flat, E, G, G.

8  Nicolai Rimsky-Korsakov: from his opera *Tsar Saltan*.

9  Violin-making. They were the leading family of violin-makers in the sixteenth century; the following century they

were joined by the Guarneri and Stradivari families, also of Cremona.

10  He invented the hammer-action pianoforte, around the year 1709.

11  Strauss. Between them the members of the family composed nearly 1,000 works, notably waltzes and polkas.

12  Peter Warlock.

13  It is wholly female. *Suor Angelica* (*Sister Angelica*) is usually performed together with the other two operas in *Il Trittico* (*The Triptych*), *Il Tabarro* (*The Cloak*) and *Gianni Schicchi*.

14  A musical instrument consisting of a series of tuned glass vessels. The notes are produced by friction, either with the fingers or mechanically.

15  Don Gillis. The work is subtitled 'A Symphony for Fun'.

16  Johann Helmich Roman, who was born in Stockholm in 1694 and died in Haraldsmåla in 1758. He wrote twenty-one symphonies, twenty violin sonatas, a number of concertos, and so on.

17  Arthur Honegger: *Pacific 231* (1924), a 'locomotive tone poem'.

18  Nicolai Rimsky-Korsakov. A setting of the poem by Pushkin, it was first produced in Moscow in 1898.

19  A series of variations for six pianofortes by Franz Liszt, Sigismond Thalberg, Heinrich Herz, Johann Peter Pixis, Carl Czerny and Frédéric Chopin, based on an aria from Bellini's opera *I Puritani*. The introduction, finale and connecting passages are by Liszt, and the whole work was first published in 1837.

20  Thomas Augustine Arne (1710–78).

21  Igor Stravinsky. It is a ballet composed in 1937.

22  Tchaikovsky. The opera was completed between the composition of his fifth and sixth symphonies.

23  An obsolete wind instrument, once much used in bands and church orchestras, which went out of favour in the nineteenth century. Its great length—some eight feet—meant that it had to be shaped in a series of sharp curves, which gave it its descriptive name.

24 Aaron Copland. The work, for speaker and orchestra, includes certain of Lincoln's speeches.

25 Ralph Vaughan Williams. This is a choral suite based on poems by John Skelton (c1460–1529).

26 Hector Berlioz: his *Symphonie funèbre et triomphale*, composed in 1840.

27 A baryton is a bowed string instrument of the bass viol type, which found favour in Germany during the eighteenth century. As the neck of the instrument was open, the strings (sympathetic) could be plucked from behind by the player's thumb as well as from in front. The baryton was greatly favoured by Prince Esterházy, and Haydn wrote nearly two hundred works for it. A baritone is a voice whose range falls roughly between those of the tenor and the bass.

28 Twenty. (Further details are given in 'The Numbers Game' in chapter 14.)

29 Animated, lively.

30 A soft-toned organ stop of the diapason type.

31 A horn made from an elephant's tusk.

32 A Spanish operetta of the lighter variety, usually in one act.

33 Conducting.

34 Thomas Tallis.

35 Both compositions—the first written in 1929 for chorus, piano and orchestra, the second in 1923—make use of jazz rhythms.

36 Cyril Smith; Rae Robertson; Victor Babin.

37 Traditional Spanish dances.

38 Odd man out here is Casals, the famous cellist; the rest were violinists.

39 The first cataloguer of Domenico Scarlatti's works; Longo (1864–1945) was also a pianist and composer of piano music. Subsequently there has been an edition by Ralph Kirkpatrick.

40 This is a colloquial term for the signs indicating a *crescendo* or a *diminuendo*.

41 Hector Berlioz.

42 Peter Cornelius (1824–74).

43 François Boïeldieu (1775–1834).

44 The eminent nineteenth-century cataloguer of Mozart's works—hence the familiar 'K' numbers.

45 Arnold Schönberg. His system abolished keys and certain notes of the scale—tonic, dominant, subdominant, mediant.

46 The String Trio No. 4 in D, op. 70 no. 1, by Beethoven.

47 *La Atlantida*, an opera completed by Ernesto Halffter.

48 Ernest Bloch (1880–1959). They are respectively a rhapsody for cello and orchestra, an orchestral work and a work for violin and piano.

49 Carmina Burana (1935–6), Catulli Carmina (1943) and Trionfi dell, Afrodite (1952), which are all cantatas.

50 Franz Liszt. It is based on the melodic motif B (B flat), A, C, H (B natural).

51 This is German for 'heroic tenor' and is usually applied to Wagnerian roles.

52 *Lied* is German for 'song'; more specifically, the term is applied to a form of German Romantic art song, normally with piano accompaniment.

53 The coloratura soprano has a wide-ranging voice of great flexibility with which she can execute interesting vocal gymnastics, trills and runs. The lyric soprano's voice is one of great sweetness and expression.

54 A male alto; the voice was popular in the sixteenth and seventeenth centuries.

55 *Basso profundo*.

56 *H.M.S. Pinafore*.

57 'The Town of Titipu' and 'The Statutory Duel'.

58 Ralph Vaughan Williams.

59 Dmitri Shostakovich; Nicolai Rimsky-Korsakov; Michael Glinka.

60 Sir Henry Wood.

61 Edward German Jones.

62 George Antheil (1900–59), in his *Ballet mécanique*.

63 Wind and thunder machines.

64 Alban Berg, in his opera *Wozzeck*.

65 Dmitri Shostakovich. It is a ballet in three acts.

66 Tchaikovsky.

67 Alfredo Casella (1883–1947).

68 International Society for Contemporary Music. Founded in 1922, the Society holds a festival in a different country each year with the object of promoting the music of contemporary composers.

69 Variations on 'God Save the King', and *Wellington's Victory or the Battle of Vittoria*, both by Beethoven, and Carl Weber's *Jubel Overture*, are perhaps the best known. (There is also a work by Charles Ives (1874–1954) that uses the same tune, entitled Variations on 'America', for organ, 1891.)

70 Emmanuel Chabrier (1841–94).

71 Emile Waldteufel (1837–1915).

72 Johann Sebastian Bach, for his most gifted pupil Johann Gottlieb Goldberg (1727–56).

73 Henry Purcell.

74 A rather elaborate ornamental type of music, usually of the seventeenth and eighteenth centuries. The term came to be applied to music by association with the highly decorated architecture of the same period.

75 Jean Barraqué, a French composer (1928–73) and pupil of Olivier Messiaen (b. 1908).

76 Franz Liszt.

77 Hans Pfitzner (1869–1949).

78 Giovanni Palestrina.

79 Johannes Brahms. The words are taken from the Bible.

80 Guiseppe Verdi. They comprise *Ave Maria*, *Stabat Mater*, *Laudi alla Vergine* and *Te Deum*.

81 Jacques Ibert (1890–1962).

82 They were all of negro descent.

83 Antonín Dvořák.

84 Norman Dello Joio (b. 1913). The work is influenced by the composer's love of Gregorian chant.

85 A vihuela is a Spanish instrument similar to a guitar, but strung and played like a lute. A viola is a member of the violin family, larger and lower in pitch than the violin itself.

86 'Là ci darem la mano' ('Give me your hand, o fairest') from *Don Giovanni*.

87  The Russian Mily Balakirev (1837–1910).

88  Alexander Scriabin. The first is an orchestral work, the second a symphonic poem requiring, according to the composer's direction, 'a keyboard of light'.

89  Jean Sibelius: incidental music to *Belshazzar's Feast*, op. 51, written for the play by Procope; and William Walton: *Belshazzar's Feast* (cantata).

90  The 'Lemminkäinen' suite (Four Legends for Orchestra, op. 22) by Sibelius.

91  Sibelius, as incidental music to Strindberg's play.

92  Christian Sinding (1856–1941).

93  Dame Ethel Smyth (1858–1944).

94  An English composer who lived from around 1495 to 1545; his works include eight Masses, twenty-eight motets, three Magnificats and other church music.

95  An English composer born in 1944, whose works include the *Requiem for Father Malachy* (1972).

96  The American Deems Taylor (1885–1966).

97  Georg Telemann (1681–1767).

98  Richard Strauss.

99  Hugo Wolf.

100  Tchaikovsky.

# 4 ART, LITERATURE AND MUSIC

## Art and Music

1 Rachmaninov: *The Isle of the Dead*, a symphonic poem, first performed 1909.
2 *Pictures from an Exhibition* (first performed 1874), later orchestrated by Ravel. The painter was Victor Hartmann.
3 Enrique Granados (1867–1916): *Goyescas*—the piano work was performed in 1914 and the opera first performed in New York in 1916. The painter was, of course, Goya (1746–1828).
4 Ottorino Respighi (1879–1936): *Three Botticelli Pictures* for small orchestra.
5 Paul Hindemith (1895–1963): *Mathis der Maler* (*Mathis the Painter*), an opera, which formed the basis of a symphony of the same name.
6 John McCabe: *The Chagall Windows*, an orchestral work, first performed 1974.

## The Bible

1 Antonín Dvořák. With the exception of the *Gipsy Songs*, op. 55, these are perhaps his best-known songs. They are a collection of ten songs for voice and piano, and were composed in New York in 1894. Dvořák later orchestrated five of them.
2 Ralph Vaughan Williams, after William Blake's illustrations. One of Vaughan Williams's most popular works, *Job* has eight scenes, each of which is prefaced with a biblical superscription. The ballet was first produced by the Carmargo Society in July 1931.
3 Joseph Haydn. First performed in Vienna, 1798, *The Creation* takes its text from *Genesis* and *Paradise Lost*. It was translated into German and later re-translated into English.
4 An opera in three acts by Arnold Schönberg (1874–1951), of

which only Acts 1 and 2 were completed. It was first performed in 1954 on Hamburg Radio.

5 Johann Kuhnau (1660–1722). They consist of six sonatas for keyboard (organ, clavichord or harpsichord), and are the earliest examples of programme music.

6 Leonard Bernstein (b. 1918). This is his first symphony and was first performed in 1944.

## May I Have a Programme?

1 *Bolero* by Maurice Ravel (1875–1937), first performed in Paris, 1928.

2 *Le Rouet d'Omphale* (*Omphale's Spinning Wheel*) by Camille Saint-Saëns (1835–1921), his first symphonic poem, composed in 1871.

3 *Night on the Bare Mountain*, sometimes known as *St John's Night on the Bare Mountain*. The original version was by Mussorgsky.

4 *Symphonie fantastique*, op. 14 by Berlioz, which was first performed in Paris on 5 December 1830. There is a sequel to this work called *Lélio ou Le Retour à la vie* (*Lélio, or the return to life*) for actor, solo voices, chorus, pianoforte and orchestra, first performed in the same programme as *Symphonie fantastique* in Paris on 9 December 1832.

5 *The Pines of Rome* by Ottorino Respighi (1879–1936); this symphonic poem was composed in 1924.

6 *The Moldau* (or *Vltava*) by Bedřich Smetana (1824–84). It is the second of a cycle of six symphonic poems under the collective title of *Má Vlast* (*My Country*), composed between 1874 and 1879.

## Drama

1 Tchaikovsky: Fantasy Overture; Berlioz: a Dramatic Symphony, op. 17; Prokofiev: a ballet, op. 64. All the pieces are entitled *Romeo and Juliet*.

2 Ambroise Thomas (1811–96): an opera; Tchaikovsky: an overture-fantasia; Berlioz: a Funeral March to the last scene;

William Walton (b. 1902): incidental music to Laurence Olivier's film. There is also a symphonic poem by Franz Liszt.

3 Edvard Grieg: *Peer Gynt*.

4 Claude Debussy: an opera; Gabriel Fauré: incidental music; Arnold Schönberg: a symphonic poem, op. 5; Jean Sibelius: incidental music; Cyril Scott (1879–1970): an overture.

5 Liszt: a symphonic poem, *Prometheus*; Beethoven: music for the ballet, *The Creatures of Prometheus*, op. 43; Alexander Scriabin (1872–1915): a symphonic poem, *Prometheus— The Poem of Fire*; Hubert Parry (1848–1918): a setting for solo voices, chorus and orchestra, *Prometheus Unbound*.

6 *La Dame aux Camélias* by Alexandre Dumas *fils*.

### Fairy Tales

1 *Skazka* is a Russian word meaning fairy tale or legend. Rimsky-Korsakov (1844–1908) wrote an orchestral work, *Skazka*, op. 29; Nicholas Medtner (1880–1951) wrote a number of *Skazki* for the piano, including his op. 14 and op. 26.

2 *The Hump-Backed Horse* or *The Tsar Maiden*.

3 Jules Massenet: *Cendrillon*, first performed in Paris, 1899; Gioacchino Rossini: *La Cenerentola*, first performed in Rome, 1817.

4 Sergei Prokofiev.

5 Benjamin Britten (1913–76). The choreography and libretto are by John Cranko, and the ballet was first performed in London in 1957.

6 *The Sleeping Beauty* by Tchaikovsky. They are all movements from the ballet.

### Films

1 Erich Korngold (1897–1957).
2 Virgil Thomson (b. 1896).
3 John Ireland (1879–1962).
4 Sir Arthur Bliss (1891–1975).

5 Sir William Walton (b. 1902): *Spitfire* Prelude and Fugue.
6 Ralph Vaughan Williams (1872–1956). Vaughan Williams subsequently wrote the *Sinfonia Antarctica*, using themes from the music he wrote for *Scott of the Antarctic*.

## Just a Few Lines . . .

1 J. S. Bach. The letter was written to Christian Ludwig, Margrave of Brandenburg, to whom Bach was submitting his *Brandenburg* Concertos. (Note the grovelling self-deprecation of this giant among composers!)
2 Niccolò Paganini (1782–1840). Paganini wrote to thank Hector Berlioz for *Harold in Italy*, which he had especially commissioned. Paganini subsequently took an intense dislike to the work.
3 Mozart. His 'sons' were the six String Quartets, K. 387, K. 421, K. 428, K. 458, K. 464 and K. 465, which were dedicated to Haydn.

## Literature and Music

1 Gustav Holst (1874–1934). Egdon Heath is the scene of Thomas Hardy's novel *The Return of the Native*.
2 Tchaikovsky: a symphony (first performed 1886); Schumann: an overture and fifteen numbers (first performed 1852).
3 Ralph Vaughan Williams: *On Wenlock Edge*, settings of poems from *A Shropshire Lad*; George Butterworth (1885–1916): *A Shropshire Lad*, a setting of six poems from Housman's work.
4 Liza Lehmann (1862–1918); the song cycle was based on Edward Fitzgerald's translation of the 'Rubáiyát of Omar Khayyám'.
5 Samuel Coleridge-Taylor (1875–1912); the three cantatas, which are for solo voices, chorus and orchestra, are *Hiawatha's Wedding Feast*, *The Death of Minnehaha* and *Hiawatha's Departure*. The poem *Hiawatha* is by the American Henry Wadsworth Longfellow (1807–82).

6 Joseph Haydn. The text was taken from Milton's *Paradise Lost* and *Genesis*, and translated into German by Gottfried van Swieten as *Die Schöpfung*.

## Myths and Legends

1 Jean Sibelius (1865–1957). The *Legends* are entitled: (1) *Lemminkäinen and the Maidens*; (2) *Lemminkäinen in Tuonela*; (3) *The Swan of Tuonela*; (4) *Lemminkäinen's Homecoming*.
2 The two legends are 'St Francis of Assisi preaching to the Birds' and 'St Francis de Paule walking on the Water'; the oratorios are *The Legend of St Elizabeth*, first performed 1865, and *The Legend of St Cecilia*, first performed 1874.
3 *Josephslegende* (*The Legend of Joseph*), which was composed in 1913–14.
4 Igor Stravinsky: *Apollo Musagètes* (*Apollo, Leader of the Muses*), composed in 1927.
5 Sir Arthur Bliss. The libretto is by J. B. Priestley, and the opera was first performed in London in 1949.
6 *Orpheus in the Underworld*, first performed 1848; *La Belle Hélène*, first produced in 1864.

## Poets' Corner

1 William Shakespeare (1564–1616): Sonnet No. VIII.
2 John Dryden (1631–1701): *A Song for St Cecilia's Day, 1687*.
3 John Milton (1608–74): *Il Penseroso*.
4 Leigh Hunt (1784–1859): *The Fancy Concert*.
5 Percy Bysshe Shelley (1794–1822): *To ——*.
6 Robert Browning (1812–89): *A Toccata of Galuppi's*.

## Sir Walter Scott and Opera

1 *La Dame Blanche* (*The White Lady*) by François Adrien Boïeldieu (1775–1834), produced in Paris in 1825.
2 *Ivanhoe*, a five-act opera by Sir Arthur Sullivan (1842–1900), produced in London, 31 January 1891.

3 *Lucia di Lammermoor* by Gaetano Donizetti (1797–1848), produced in Naples, 26 September 1835.
4 *I Puritani di Scozia* (*The Scottish Puritans*) by Vincenzo Bellini (1801–35), produced in Paris, 24 January 1835.
5 *La jolie fille de Perth* (*The Fair Maid of Perth*) by Georges Bizet (1838–75), produced in Paris, 26 December 1867.
6 *La Donna del Lago* by Gioacchino Rossini (1792–1863), produced in Naples, 24 September 1819.

## Witches, Goblins and Fairies

1 *The Noonday Witch*.
2 *The Water Goblin*.
3 *The Witches' Sabbath*.
4 *The Fairy Queen*.
5 Peter Warlock.
6 *Le baiser de la fée* (*The Fairy's Kiss*).

# 5 FARAWAY PLACES

## Capital Cities

1 Respighi: *The Fountains of Rome* and *The Pines of Rome.*
2 Delius: *Paris: The Song of a Great City.*
3 Walton: *Johannesburg Festival Overture, 1956.*
4 Prague; Mozart's Symphony No. 38 in D, K. 504.
5 *Wiener Blut* (*Vienna Blood*) by Johann Strauss the younger (1825–99).
6 *Carillon de Westminster* by Louis Vierne (1870–1937), who, blind from birth, was organist of Notre Dame, Paris.

## First Produced in London

1 Benjamin Britten (1913–76): New Theatre, February 1939.
2 Roger Quilter (1877–1953): Savoy Theatre, 1911.
3 Sir Edward Elgar (1857–1934): Kingsway Theatre, December 1915.
4 Gabriel Fauré (1845–1924), orchestrated by Charles Koechlin (1867–1950): Prince of Wales Theatre, 1898.
5 Frederick Delius (1862–1934): His Majesty's Theatre, September 1923.
6 Benjamin Britten: Mercury Theatre, February 1937.

## Folk Songs and Dances in Music

1 *The Little Birch Tree.*
2 *Stenka Razin*, op. 13. The work is based on the tune *Ey Ukhnem* (*Song of the Volga Boatmen*).
3 Farandole. *L'Arlésienne* by Alphonse Daudet, produced in 1872.
4 Isaac Albéniz (1860–1909), Enrique Granados (1867–1916), Manuel de Falla (1876–1946) and Joaquin Turina (1882–

1949) are probably the most important Spanish composers to use the folk element in their music.

5 Ralph Vaughan Williams (1872–1958); for military band.
6 Percy Grainger (1882–1961).

## España

1 Édouard Lalo (1823–92). This is, in effect, a five-movement violin concerto, although the first two movements are often omitted. It was dedicated to Pablo de Sarasate, who gave its first performance in Paris in 1875.
2 Maurice Ravel (1875–1937). An opera in one act that was first produced in Paris in 1911.
3 Maurice Ravel. A one-movement orchestral suite, first performed 1907.
4 Emmanuel Chabrier (1841–94). A rhapsody for orchestra, first performed in Paris, 1883.
5 Nicolai Rimsky-Korsakov. A symphonic suite, based on themes from Spanish 'folk-songs'. It was first performed in 1887.
6 Sir Edward Elgar (1857–1934). An uncompleted opera begun in 1932–3.

## Heavenly Music

1 *The Triumph of Neptune*, which was first performed in London, 1926.
2 The movements are: 'Mars the bringer of war', 'Venus the bringer of peace', 'Mercury the winged messenger', 'Jupiter the bringer of jollity', 'Saturn the bringer of old age', 'Uranus the magician' and 'Neptune the mystic'. The work is, of course, *The Planets*.
3 'E lucevan le stelle', which comes from Act 3 of Puccini's *Tosca*.
4 *Jupiter*. This was not the composer's name for the symphony.
5 *The Moon and Sixpence* by W. Somerset Maugham. The opera was first performed in 1957.
6 *Sphärenklänge waltz* (*Music of the spheres*) by Josef Strauss.

## London

1 *Cockaigne* Overture op. 40, composed in 1901.
2 These are Haydn's last twelve symphonies, which were written for the London impresario Johann Peter Salomon who first brought Haydn to London in 1791. The symphonies are numbered 93–104, the last, in D, being nicknamed the *London* Symphony.
3 Gustav Holst (1874–1934). The suite for string orchestra was written in 1913 for the girls of St Paul's School, London, where Holst was musical director from 1905 until the end of his life.
4 Eric Coates (1886–1957). The first was the *London Suite*, composed in 1932; the second was the suite *London Again*, which was composed in 1936.
5 Sir William Walton (b. 1902). Incidentally, the famous work mentioned in the question is *Façade—an entertainment*, with twenty-one poems written by Edith Sitwell.
6 Ralph Vaughan Williams (1872–1958): Symphony No. 2, first performed 1914, revised version, 1920.

## National Anthems

1 Claude Joseph Rouget de Lisle (1760–1836), a captain in the engineers, who composed the words and music on the night of 24 April 1792 after the mayor of Strasbourg had been heard regretting that the young soldiers had no patriotic song to sing as they marched.
2 Belgium. It was written and composed at the time of the revolution of 1830.
3 *Soldier's Song* (*'seo dhibh, a chairde*). Written by Peadar Kearney, the uncle of Brendan Behan, it was composed in 1907, published in 1912 and officially adopted in 1926.
4 *God Save the King* (*Queen*). It is a tune whose ancient origin cannot be precisely identified, and it cannot be attributed to any one composer.
5 Joseph Haydn. As *Gott erhalte Franz den Kaiser* this was the national hymn of Austria from 1797 when Haydn composed it

until 1918 when Austria became a republic and adopted the Österreichische bundes hymne—*Sei gesegnet ohne Ende* (*Thine be never-ending blessings*).

6 *Slavonic march* (*Marche Slave*), op. 31, which was composed during the Russo-Turkish War (1827–9) for a concert in aid of wounded soldiers.

## Italy

1 Hugo Wolf (1860–1903).
2 Peter Ilich Tchaikovsky (1840–93).
3 Gustave Charpentier (1860–1956).
4 Hugo Wolf.
5 Hector Berlioz (1803–69).
6 Felix Mendelssohn (1809–47).

## We Love Paris

1 *La Vie Parisienne*. An opera first performed in 1866.
2 *An American in Paris*. A descriptive piece for orchestra, including four taxi-horns, first performed 1928.
3 Symphony No. 31 in D major, K. 297, *Paris*. Written in Paris in 1778.
4 *Gaîté Parisienne*. A one-act ballet choreographed by Leonid Massine and first performed by the Ballet Russe de Monte Carlo in Monte Carlo in April 1938.
5 *Carnival in Paris*. This 'episode' for orchestra (1879) and Svendsen's Romance for violin and orchestra are the most popular of this Norwegian-born composer's works.
6 *Paris: The Song of a Great City*.

# 6 A MUSICAL DETECTIVE STORY

For the detective it was elementary.
1 *The Barber of Baghdad* is the overture to the opera of the same name (first performed in Weimar, 1858) by Peter Cornelius (1824–74). Rossini, of course, wrote the famous overture to the opera *The Barber of Seville*, which received its first performance in Rome in 1816.
2 Bach's *Italian* Concerto is for solo harpsichord or piano; it was not scored for orchestral accompaniment.
3 *Swan White* was composed by Sibelius, his op. 54, and is the incidental music to a play by Strindberg. The suspect perhaps confused it with the well-known ballet by Tchaikovsky, *Swan Lake*.
4 César Franck composed only one symphony; it is not numbered and is known simply as 'Symphony in D minor'.

# 7 SAINTS AND SINNERS

## Devilish Music

1 Giuseppe Tartini (1692–1770). He called his Sonata in G minor for violin and continuo the *Devil's Trill* Sonata because it was, he said, played to him by Satan in a dream.
2 Arthur Benjamin (1893–1960). His opera *The Devil Take Her* was first produced at the Royal College of Music, London, in 1931.
3 Claude Debussy (1862–1918). This uncompleted opera (1903), which had a libretto by Debussy, was based on a story by Edgar Allan Poe.
4 *Mephisto* Waltzes: Nos. 1 and 2 were written for orchestra and later transcribed for piano; Nos. 3 and 4 were written for piano.
5 *Mefistofele*. The first performance of the opera, at La Scala, Milan, 1868, ended in a riot and, after two subsequent performances, was withdrawn by the management on the orders of the Chief of Police. Boito later revised the opera's length and orchestration, and it gradually achieved great popularity.
6 Antonín Dvořák. In this three-act opera, op. 112, which he began in 1898 and completed in 1899, Dvořák made extensive use of Slavonic folk music.

## Saints and Sinners

1 *St John* (first performed Good Friday, 1723), *St Matthew* (first performed Good Friday, 1729) and *St Mark* (first performed Good Friday, 1731). (Although the *St Luke* Passion is included in the edition of Bach's collected works published in Leipzig 1851–1900, it is thought not to be by Bach.)
2 *St Paul*. The oratorio was completed in 1836, and the text was taken from the Bible.

3  Gioacchino Rossini (1792–1868). This was the name given by
   the composer to several sets of songs and instrumental pieces,
   after he had given up composing operas.
4  Kurt Weill (1900–50) with Bertold Brecht (1898–1955). The
   opera was written in Paris in 1936.
5  Henry Purcell (1659–95): *Ode to Saint Cecilia*; Benjamin
   Britten (1913–76): *Hymn to Saint Cecilia*.
6  Virgil Thomson (b. 1896). This opera, which does, in fact,
   have four acts, was first produced in 1934.

# 8  GRAMOPHONE QUIZ

1  Thomas Edison (1847–1931), Émile Berliner (1851–1929) and Alexander Graham Bell (1847–1922).
2  'E lucevan le stelle' from Puccini's *Tosca*.
3  The Original Dixieland Jazz Band; the recording was made in 1917.
4  The famous dog, featured with a trumpet on the HMV–RCA Victor logo; it was taken from the painting by Louis Barraud.
5  'Nipper' was listening to an Edison Cylinder Phonograph in Barraud's painting.
6  They are all well-known American record reviewers and have written books on the gramophone.
7  An eminent producer, latterly an executive with CBS records, and a stalwart in the gramophone record industry. He was born in England but subsequently adopted American citizenship.
8  12 August 1877
9  Thomas Edison.
10  Cardboard covered with tinfoil.
11  1887; Berliner's invention was the lateral-cut flat record, from which the word gramophone was coined.
12  The pianist Josef Hofmann (1876–1957), who was then only twelve years old.
13  The Gramophone Company, later known as 'His Master's Voice'.
14  1926.
15  1902.
16  Landon Ronald (1873–1938).
17  Recording was done acoustically by the artists performing in front of a large (usually) papier mâché horn, which carried their sounds to the stylus of the disc-cutter and thence to the waxed surface.

18 1931; the record was a 33⅓ r.p.m. microgroove, but it was never marketed commercially as there were no pick-ups at the time capable of playing it.

19 1948, released by RCA Victor.

20 June 1950, for the Decca Record Company.

21 1958.

22 It is one continuous groove.

23 1965.

24 The eight-track cartridge.

25 A noise reduction system that greatly helped the acceptance of the musicassette as a truly hi-fi medium.

26 He perfected, in 1931, the stereo recording technique as we know it today.

27 *God Save the King* on a disc measuring one inch in diameter. It was made for Queen Mary's dolls' house, and plays one verse.

28 Full Frequency Range Recording; the system was perfected by the Decca Record Company.

29 *The Lord's Prayer* recorded by Émile Berliner on a cylinder and still preserved in the archives of the BBC record library.

30 Dame Nellie Melba (1861–1931).

31 A French poet who devised a method of recording sound in a groove on a lamp-blackened glass disc in 1877.

32 The Gramophone and Typewriter Company.

33 The recording of Tchaikovsky's First Piano Concerto on RCA by Van Cliburn (b. 1934).

34 Beethoven's Symphony No. 5 in C minor, recorded by Arthur Nikisch and the Berlin Philharmonic Orchestra.

35 Verticle- or lateral-cut discs, introduced by Pathé in 1906. They were sometimes played from the centre to the ring.

36 It is a system of recording which measures the shape of the sound so that it is then stored as a series of numbers, with the result that, when these numbers are converted back to sound, they do not become distorted. The overall advantage of this system is that there are fewer extraneous background noises, and no fluctuations in speed.

37 King George V and Queen Mary.

38 Paul Whiteman and his Ambassador Orchestra.

39  A console gramophone with horn facing downwards, stand-
    ing about four feet high.
40  Odeon and Fonotipia.
41  1903; Italian HMV released Verdi's *Ernani* on forty single-
    sided discs.
42  Grand Prix du Disque; Edison Award; N.A.R.A.S. Grammy
    Award.
43  1923.
44  Sir Compton Mackenzie.
45  Brahms: String Quartet No. 1 in C minor, op. 51, no. 1,
    played by the Catterall Quartet. The record was issued in
    1923.
46  September 1920.
47  December 1920.
48  The bugler who sounded the original charge was recorded on
    this cylinder with the original bugle.
49  Fonotipia, which began life in 1904.
50  An engineer who provided the gramophone with its first
    motor, developed the recording process, and, in partnership
    with Émile Berliner, launched the Victor Talking Machine
    Company, later known as RCA Victor.

# 9 BALLET, OPERA AND OPERETTA

## Ballet Music

1 Peter Ilich Tchaikovsky (1840–93), Maurice Ravel (1875–1937) and Manuel de Falla (1876–1946). The music was all written for the ballet stage but later became popular in concert form.
2 Claude Debussy (1862–1913); Nicolai Rimsky-Korsakov (1844–1908). Both pieces were written for the concert platform and later used for ballets by Nijinsky and Fokine.
3 Among others, Diaghilev commissioned Igor Stravinsky, Manuel de Falla, Darius Milhaud and Francis Poulenc.
4 *Checkmate*: Sir Arthur Bliss (1891–1975). The ballet was first performed by Sadler's Wells Ballet at the Champs-Elysées Theatre in Paris on 15 June 1937.
5 *Pineapple Poll*. This was first performed by Sadler's Wells Ballet at Sadler's Wells on 13 March 1951.
6 *La Source* (*Naïla*); first performed Paris, 1866.

## Mr Gilbert and Mr Sullivan

1 Strictly speaking it was *Thespis* (1871), but the manuscript was lost or destroyed.
2 *The Grand Duke or, The Statutory Duel*, which was first performed in London, 1896.
3 *Cox and Box*, first performed in London, 1867. The libretto is by F. C. Burnand.
4 *The Emerald Isle*, first performed in London, 1901.
5 *The Gondoliers*. The operetta was first performed in London in 1889, and was Gilbert and Sullivan's last successful collaboration.
6 *The Peer and the Peri*. The operetta was first performed in London and in New York on the same day in 1882.

## Opera

1 Susanna was a secret smoker in the opera by Ermanno Wolf-Ferrari (1876–1948), *Il Segreto di Susanna* (*Susanna's Secret*), first performed in Munich, 4 December 1909.

2 Domenico Cimarosa (1749–1801): the opera is *Il Matrimonio Segreto* (*The Secret Marriage*), first performed 1792. The hero and heroine, named in the question, are secretly married.

3 Minnie, in Puccini's three-act opera *La Fanciulla del West* (*The Girl of the Golden West*). Minnie tries to save the life of Dick Johnson, her bandit lover, by playing a game of poker with the sheriff, Jack Rance. She cheats, by hiding some cards in her stocking and wins the game and consequently saves the life of her lover.

4 In Act 2 of Puccini's *Turandot*, the Princess Turandot asks Calaf the following riddles: (1) 'What is the phantom that is born every night and dies every day?' Calaf correctly replies: 'It is what now inspires me: it is hope.' (2) 'What is it that at times is like a fever, yet grows cold when you die; that blazes up if you think of great deeds?' Calaf correctly answers: 'It is the blood.' (3) 'What is the ice that sets you on fire?' Once again Calaf has the correct answer: 'You are the ice that sets me on fire,' i.e., the answer is Turandot. After this ordeal Turandot is still unwilling to marry Calaf, who agrees to release her from her vow if she can discover the secret of his name. She fails, and Calaf claims her hand. No longer unwilling, Turandot declares that the stranger's true name is Love.

5 Amfortas in *Parsifal*.

6 Opera is usually assumed to have begun in 1600 with *Eurydice* by Jacopo Peri (1561–1633), which is acknowledged as the first surviving opera; a previous opera by the same composer (*Daphne*, 1597) is now lost.

# 10 MORNING, NOON AND NIGHT

## The Four Elements

1 *Das Lied von der Erde* (*The Song of the Earth*), first performed 1911.
2 Alexander Scriabin (1872–1915).
3 From the ballet *The Rite of Spring* by Igor Stravinsky. When it was first performed in Paris in 1913 it caused a riot.
4 The three 'symphonic sketches' *La mer* (*The Sea*), first performed 1905; two pieces for piano, *Reflets dans l'eau* (*Reflections in the Water*) and *Jardins sous la pluie* (*Gardens in the Rain*).
5 Ralph Vaughan Williams (1872–1958): Symphony No. 7, *Sinfonia Antarctica*. The symphony, first performed in 1953, was based on the music he had written for the film *Scott of the Antarctic* (1949).
6 This is the nickname given to Haydn's Symphony No. 59 in A major.

## Humour

1 *Ein Musikalischer Spass* (*A Musical Joke*) in F major, K. 522. It is also occasionally known as *Dorfmusik* (*The Village Band*)
2 *Háry János*, an opera by Zoltán Kodály (1882–1967), containing popular Hungarian tunes and first produced in Budapest in 1926. Kodály later arranged a successful orchestral suite from the material, which was first performed in 1927.
3 Antonín Dvořák: *Eight Humoresques*, op. 101 (1894); Robert Schumann: *Humoreske*, op. 20 in B flat (1839).
4 *The Good-humoured Ladies*. The ballet, which was choreographed by Leonid Massine, was first produced in Rome in 1917.

5 Gustav Holst (1874–1934). He wrote his own libretto, and the opera parodies the operatic idiosyncrasies and mannerisms of certain composers. Holst later made a successful orchestral suite of several items from the opera.

6 Camille Saint-Saëns (1835–1921): *The Carnival of Animals*; Saint-Saëns parodies his *Danse Macabre* in the twelfth section, 'Fossils'.

## Morning, Noon and Night

1 Franz von Suppe (1819–95).

2 Joseph Haydn (1732–1809): Symphonies No. 6 in D major, No. 7 in C major and No. 8 in G major, all of which were written in about 1761.

3 Claude Debussy: *Prélude à l'Après-midi d'un faune* (*Prelude to the Afternoon of a Faun*). The name of the dancer is Nijinsky, and the ballet was first produced by the Ballets Russes in Paris in 1912.

4 Jean Sibelius (1865–1957).

5 Edvard Grieg (1843–1907): 'Morning' from the first *Peer Gynt* suite.

6 Felix Mendelssohn: incidental music, including the famous Wedding March, written in 1842; Benjamin Britten: an opera, first produced at Aldeburgh in 1960.

## Oh Death Where is Thy Sting? (1)

1 Philip Heseltine, who adopted the pseudonym Peter Warlock. He was born in 1894, and is perhaps best known for his songs.

2 Jean-Baptiste Lully. Born in Italy in 1632, he died in the church of St Roch in Paris on 22 March 1687 while conducting a Te Deum.

3 Alban Berg. He was born in Vienna in 1885 and died there on 24 December 1935.

4 Ernest Chausson. Born in Paris in 1855, he died on his own estate near Mantes-sur-Seine on 10 June 1899.

5  César Franck. He was born at Liège in 1822, dying in Paris on 8 November 1890.
6  Eduard Strauss. Born in Vienna in 1835, he died there on 28 December 1916.

## Oh Death Where is They Sting? (2)

1  *Otello* (*The Moor of Venice*) by Verdi; first performed at La Scala, Milan, in 1887. The libretto was adapted from Shakespeare's play by Boito.
2  *Wozzeck* by Alban Berg; first produced in Berlin on 14 December 1925. The opera is based on a play by Georg Büchner, and the libretto is by the composer.
3  *La Traviata* by Verdi; first produced in Venice on 6 March 1853. The story is taken from *La Dame aux Camélias* by Dumas *fils*.
4  *Carmen* by Bizet; first produced in Paris on 3 March 1875. The libretto was by Meilhac and Halévy, based on the novel by Prosper Mérimée.
5  *Salome* by Richard Strauss; first produced on 9 December 1905 in Dresden. It is interesting to note that the eroticism of the music and the text, which was by Oscar Wilde, caused the Kaiser in Berlin, the Lord Chamberlain in London and various churches in the United States to condemn the opera as obscene, and some performances were cancelled because of puritanical criticism.
6  *Don Giovanni* (*Don Juan*) by Mozart, first produced on 7 May 1787 in Prague. The libretto is by da Ponte.

## The Seasons

1  Cécile Chaminade (1857–1944). Although she wrote several orchestra suites, trios, a ballet and songs, she is known today chiefly by *Autumn*, op. 35, and by *Autrefois*, op. 87.
2  Benjamin Britten (1913–76). It was first performed in Holland in 1949.
3  Frédéric Chopin (1810–49). It is the nickname of the A minor *étude*, op. 25, no. 11.

4 Frederick Delius (1862–1934). They are all orchestral works.
5 Joseph Haydn (1732–1809). *The Seasons* was his last oratorio, composed between 1798 and 1801. He was persuaded to write it following the success of *The Creation*.
6 Antonio Vivaldi (1678–1741). They are four concertos for violin and orchestra from *The Conflict Between Harmony and Invention*, op. 8, which consists of twelve concertos. However, it is *The Four Seasons* above all that have ensured lasting fame for Vivaldi.

## Weddings

1 Bedřich Smetana (1824–84): *The Bartered Bride*. The opera was first produced in Prague in 1866.
2 Carl Goldmark (1830–1915): the *Rustic Wedding* Symphony. The symphony, in five movements, was first performed in 1876.
3 Edvard Grieg (1843–1907): *Wedding Day at Troldhaugen*, from *Lyric Pieces*, op. 65, no.6.
4 Camille Saint-Saëns (1835–1921): *Wedding Cake Caprice*.
5 Sir Michael Tippett (b. 1905). The opera was first produced at Covent Garden in January 1955.
6 J. S. Bach: Cantata No. 196, *Der Herr denket an uns*. The cantata was possibly written in 1708 for the wedding of Bach's friend Lorenz Stauber.

# 11 LIGHTNING QUIZ

1 Wolfgang Amadeus Mozart.
2 They (Vrenchen and Sali) took *A Walk to the Paradise Garden*. This orchestral interlude occurs in the opera *A Village Romeo and Juliet* by Delius. The libretto, by the composer, was based on a story by Gottfried Kellerand, and in German is entitled *Romeo und Julia auf dem Dorfe*. It was first produced in Berlin in February 1907.
3 Maria Callas (1923–77).
4 Joan Sutherland (b. 1926).
5 Robert Schumann (1810–56). The pieces come from his *Carnaval*, op. 9, a set of twenty-one piano pieces (1834–5).
6 Franz Schubert (1797–1828).
7 Edvard Grieg (1843–1907).
8 In the sixteenth century a complete set of viols of various sizes—usually six instruments—was usually kept in a chest or cupboard. The viol family preceded and for a period remained contemporary with the violin family.
9 Otherwise known as a 'marine trumpet', this is an obsolete primitive string instrument, employing a single string and played with a bow.
10 William Crotch (1775–1847).
11 *Lélio ou Le Retour à la vie* is a lyric monodrama by Hector Berlioz. It is scored for an actor, solo voices, chorus, piano and orchestra, and was composed in 1831 as a sequel to his *Symphonie fantastique*.
12 It is the system of keys on woodwind instruments to facilitate accurate intonation. It was introduced by the flautist Theobold Boehm (1793–1881), and has been applied to the oboe, clarinet and bassoon as well as the flute.
13 Gioacchino Rossini (1792–1868). It was first performed in Naples, 1816, and has a libretto by de Salsa.

14  Charles Henri Valentin Alkan, real name Morhange (1813–88), French composer and pianist.

15  In *Don Giovanni* (Act 2, Scene 5) Don Giovanni and Leporello hear an aria from *Le Nozze di Figaro*.

16  Malcolm Williamson (from 1975); Sir Arthur Bliss (1953–75); Sir Arnold Bax (1942–53).

17  *Die Königin von Saba* (*The Queen of Sheba*) first produced in Vienna, 1875; *Das Heimchen am Herd* (*The Cricket on the Hearth*), first produced 1896.

18  Giuseppe Verdi (1813–1901). It was his first opera, and was first produced in 1839.

19  Arrigo Boito (1842–1918). Among his best known libretti are those for Verdi's *Falstaff* and *Otello*.

20  The opera *Intermezzo* by Richard Strauss has a libretto by the composer which is largely autobiographical, based on an episode in the composer's life. It was first produced in Dresden in 1924.

# 12 THE OLD CURIOSITY SHOP

## The Old Curiosity Shop (1)

1 An upright, instead of horizontal, harpsichord or spinet.
2 Claviorganum.
3 An 'orchestrion'. There are many automatic instruments of this kind under a number of different patented names.
4 *Sports et Divertissements* by Erik Satie (1866–1925).
5 The name is often applied wrongly to a street piano, but it is really the equivalent of the French *vielle* and the medieval name for it was 'organistrum'. The strings are made to vibrate by a wheel operated by a handle. The tune is played on the top string by means of keys set vertically to the strings. The lower strings provide a bass.
6 William Crotch (1775–1847). He was a Doctor of Music at Oxford University and organist of Christ Church. A composer of a considerable number of choral works, including the oratorio *Palestine*, he was also a graphic artist of considerable sensibility.

## The Old Curiosity Shop (2)

1 A 'Jingling Johnny' or 'Turkish Crescent', probably better known as the 'Chinese Pavilion', is a Turkish instrument that came to Europe in the eighteenth century and was used mainly by military bands. It consists of a rod with a large conical top to which is attached a crescent; from this hang a number of bells and occasionally decorations. The performer shakes the instrument causing the jingling sound.
2 Concerto for Bass Tuba and Orchestra in F minor (1954); Romance in D flat for Harmonica, String Orchestra and Piano (1951).
3 Frederick II (Frederick the Great), King of Prussia (1712–

86). He was also a flautist and composed over 120 instrumental works in many of which the flute featured prominently.

4 A brass wind instrument with a double reed invented by a French bandmaster named Sarrus in 1856. It is made in various sizes and is rarely used except in France.

5 Antonín Dvořák (1841–1904).

6 Lord Berners (Gerald Hugh Tyrwhitt-Wilson; 1883–1950).

### The Old Spuriosity Shop

1 The waltz was composed not by Weber but by Karl Gottlieb Reissiger (1798–1859), and is No. 5 of his *Danses brillantes*, op. 26.

2 Written by the German composer Gottfried Stoelzel (1690–1749).

3 This song was certainly composed by Arne though not by Thomas Augustine (1710–78) of *Rule, Britannia* fame, but by his illegitimate son Michael (1741–86).

4 The symphony is part of a longer work by Leopold Mozart (1719–87), father of Wolfgang Amadeus. It is possible that the toy instruments were added by Michael Haydn (1737–1806), brother of Joseph.

5 This was not composed by the celebrated Giovanni Battista Martini (1705–84), but by Giovanni Paolo Martini, the nom de plume of Johann Paul Aegidius Schwartzendorf (1741–1816), known as *Martini il Tedesco* (the German Martini), a German organist and composer who settled in France.

6 This symphony, discovered in Jena in 1910 and inscribed 'par Louis van Beethoven', was proved in 1957 to be the work of Jeremiah Friedrich Witt (1771–1837), an Austrian composer of orchestral and church music.

# 13 MISCELLANEOUS

## A-hunting We Will Go

1 John Bull (*c* 1562–1628). *The King's Hunt* is his best-known composition and depicts the hunt in full cry.
2 César Franck (1822–90). *Le Chasseur Maudit* (*The accursed huntsman*) is based on a German poem by G. A. Bürger and was first performed in 1882.
3 The scene is *The Royal Hunt and Storm* from Act 2 of the second part of *Les Troyens* (*The Trojans*). The libretto by Berlioz is based on Virgil's *Aeneid*.
4 Iain Hamilton (b. 1922), a Scottish composer. The libretto of the opera is after Peter Schaffer's play of the same name.
5 Symphony No. 73 in D (1781). The nickname was given to the work because of the horns and oboes in the last movement, which had previously appeared in one of Haydn's operas. *The Hunt* Quartet is op. 1 no. 1 in B flat, and is so called because of the 'horn call' in the first movement.
6 Quartet No. 17 in B flat, K. 458, *The Hunt* or *Jagdquartett*, more frequently known as *La Chasse*; it was so nicknamed because of the 'hunting' character of the opening movement.

## Abbreviations

1 Associate of the Royal Academy of Music; Associate of the Royal College of Music; Associate of the Royal College of Organists.
2 London Philharmonic Orchestra; Scottish National Orchestra; Royal Liverpool Philharmonic Orchestra.
3 Bachelor of Music; Doctor of Music; Guildhall School of Music.
4 Oboe; Obbligato; Opus.
5 Graduate of the Royal Northern College of Music; American

Society of Composers, Authors and Publishers; Mechanical
Copyright Protection Society.
6 Electrical Musical Industries; Society for the Promotion of
New Music; Incorporated Society of Musicians.

## Alternative Titles

1 *Coppélia*. First performed Paris, 1870.
2 *La Cenerentola* (*Cinderella*). First performed Rome, 1817.
3 *Così fan tutte*. First performed Vienna, 1790.
4 *Fidelio* by Beethoven.
5 *La Fille mal gardée*. First performed Paris, 1828.
6 *Carnaval: Scènes mignonnes*. This is a set of twenty-one
piano pieces built largely round the notes A–S–C–H, which
represent the name of a Bohemian town where Schumann met
a lady friend.

## Baroque

1 Approximately the seventeenth and the first half of the eighteenth centuries.
2 François Couperin (1668–1733), known as 'le Grand' to distinguish him from the nine other members of the family active
in Paris music in the seventeenth and eighteenth centuries.
3 It is derived from the Spanish *barrueco*—a strangely shaped
pearl and thence, by extension, anything thought bizarre (eg
baroque architecture). To the modern listener, most baroque
music sounds tuneful and anything but bizarre.
4 A 440—i.e., at 440 cycles per second—which was adopted as
early as 1834 by a congress of physicists, and is known as the
'Stuttgart pitch'. It is now the standard pitch.
5 'Bel canto', which literally translated means 'beautiful song';
it is the so-called Italian 'cantabile' method of singing.
6 Over 550—probably closer to 600. These were originally
published as 'esercizi per gravicembalo' or 'pieces for the cla-
vecin', or simply 'harpsichord lessons'. They initiated the
modern free style of pianoforte composition, and led to
modern systems of fingering and pianoforte technique
generally. They are now more commonly known as sonatas.

## Battle Music

1 *The Battle of Prague*. The work, which is the only piece for which Kotzwara is remembered, became very popular. Mark Twain heard it in a Lucerne hotel played by an American woman who 'turned on all the horrors of *The Battle of Prague*'.

2 *La Battaglia di Legnano* (*The Battle of Legnano*). First produced Rome, 1849.

3 *Hunnenschlacht* (*Battle of the Huns*). First performed 1857.

4 *Alexander Nevsky*, Cantata op. 78; the battle in question is *The Battle on the Ice*. First performed Moscow, 1939.

5 *The Legend of the Invisible City of Kitezh*; the battle scene is called *The Battle of Kerzhents*. First produced St Petersburg, 1907.

6 *Wellingtons Sieg* (*Wellington's Victory* or *The Battle of Victoria*). Although it was composed for performance by Mälzel's 'mechanical orchestra', it was actually performed in Vienna in 1813 by a real orchestra for the benefit of Austrian soldiers injured in the battle.


## Christmas Music

1 J. S. Bach (1685–1750). The Oratorio originally comprised six cantatas for separate performances between Christmas and Epiphany and was never intended to be performed as one work.

2 Arcangelo Corelli (1653–1713). His Concerto Grosso, op. 6 no. 8 for strings and continuo is so named; the score was inscribed 'for Christmas night', and was intended for use in church. Giuseppe Torelli (1658–1709). His Concerto Grosso, op. 8 no. 6 has the same name.

3 Victor Hely-Hutchinson (1901–47). It is the South African-born composer's best-known work.

4 Benjamin Britten (1913–76). Written in 1942, it is an arrangement of nine medieval carols for treble voices and harp.

5 Arthur Honegger (1892–1955). The piece was composed in 1953.

6 Ralph Vaughan Williams (1872–1958).

**Dedicated to You**

1 Elgar's *Enigma* Variations. Each of the fourteen sections is dedicated to the person whose initials head the section: C.A.E.: Caroline Alice Elgar (Elgar's wife); H.D.S.-P.: H.D. Stewart-Powell (amateur pianist); R.B.T.: R. B. Townshend (author); W.M.B.: W. M. Baker (country squire); R.P.A.: R. P. Arnold (son of Matthew Arnold); Ysobel: Isabel Fitton (amateur viola player); Troyte: A. Troyte Griffith (architect); W.N.: Winifred Norbury; Nimrod: A. J. Jaeger (member of Novello's staff); Dorabella: Dora Penny; G.R.S.: G. R. Sinclair (organist, Hereford Cathedral); B.G.N.: B. G. Nevison (amateur cellist); ***: Lady Mary Lygon; E.D.U.: 'Edu' (Lady Elgar's name for the composer).
2 His Bagatelle in A minor, entitled *Für Elise*.
3 Queen Victoria. The work was begun in 1831 and completed in 1842.
4 Johannes Brahms (1833–97).
5 Frederick II, the Great, of Prussia. In 1747, during Bach's visit to Potsdam, the king had given him the subject on which to extemporise.
6 Gabriel Fauré (1845–1924). Fauré, who was Ravel's teacher, was not exactly enamoured with the last movement, which he found 'stunted, badly balanced . . . in fact a failure'.

**Innovators**

1 *Parthenia* (1611). It contained music by Byrd, Bull and Orlando Gibbons.
2 Ludovico Giustini di Pistoia. Twelve sonatas were published in Florence in 1732.
3 Erik Satie (1866–1925). He introduced the typewriter in the score of his ballet *Parade* (1910).
4 It is generally accepted to have been the violinist John Bannister, at his house in Whitefriars, London, in 1672.
5 The family of Arnold Dolmetsch (1858–1940).
6 John Spencer Curwen (1816–80). Tonic Sol-fa.

## Instruments of the Orchestra

1 Flutes, piccolos, oboes, cor anglais, clarinets and bassoons.
2 Trumpets, horns, trombones, tubas and occasionally a saxophone.
3 Timpani, bass drum, side drum, cymbals, triangle, tam tam, tambourine, castanets, whip, maracas, gourd, claves, xylophone, vibraphone, glockenspiel, tubular bells, celeste, etc.
4 Forty-seven.
5 Violins, violas, cellos and double basses.
6 The oboe. A.

## Invitation to the Dance

1 *Un Ballo in Maschera*. First produced in Rome in 1859, it is considered one of the most successful of Verdi's middle-period operas.
2 *The Haunted Ballroom*. First produced at Sadler's Wells, 1934.
3 *Graduation Ball*. First performed by the Ballets Russes de Monte Carlo in Sydney, Australia, in February 1940.
4 *Amelia goes to the Ball*.
5 *Invitation to the Dance*.
6 *Di Ballo*.

## The King of Instruments

1 Albert Schweitzer (1875–1965). The composer was J. S. Bach, whose organ works Schweitzer and Widor edited.
2 Gabriel Pierné (1863–1937). He remained 'titulaire' until 1898, when he was succeeded by Charles Tournemire.
3 Any of the following would do although there are others: Willis, Harrison or Walker from England; Clicquot or Cavaillé-Coll from France; Silbermann from Germany.
4 E. Power Biggs (b. 1906).
5 Edwin H. Lemare (1865–1934). His Andantino in D flat was later turned into the popular song *Moonlight and Roses*.
6 There is a giant striding figure in the pedal part.

## Monarchs

1 Camille Saint-Saëns (1835–1921). This four-act opera, first performed in Paris in 1898, had no connection with the Shakespeare plot.
2 Edward German (1862–1936). They formed part of the incidental music to Shakespeare's play, but are often heard separately.
3 *Romeo and Juliet*, a 'dramatic symphony', op. 17 by Hector Berlioz.
4 Jean Sibelius (1865–1957). It is the incidental music to a play by Adolf Paul, composed in 1898.
5 Peter Ilich Tchaikovsky (1840–93). It was first performed in St Petersburg in 1890.
6 Eric Coates (1886–1957). Composed in 1944. As the title implies, the music depicts three queens of England.

## The Numbers Game

1 Four: *Das Rheingold, Die Walküre, Siegfried* and *Götterdämmerung*. The work was performed as a complete cycle for the first time in Bayreuth, Germany, in 1876.
2 Symphony No. 8 in E flat (1907) by Gustav Mahler. It is so called because of the enormous forces that Mahler calls for: an orchestra of 130 players, eight vocal soloists, two choirs and a children's choir numbering 400; in addition, various solo instruments are employed, including the harmonium, organ and piano.
3 Fourteen. In chronological order they are: *Thespis* (1871); *Trial by Jury* (1875); *The Sorcerer* (1877); *H.M.S. Pinafore* (1878); *The Pirates of Penzance* (1879); *Patience* (1881): *Iolanthe* (1882); *Princess Ida* (1884); *The Mikado* (1885); *Ruddigore* (1887) *The Yeoman of the Guard* (1888); *The Gondoliers* (1889); *Utopia Limited* (1893); *The Grand Duke* (1896).
4 The remarkable total of twenty, of which seven were born to Bach's first wife, Maria Barbara, who was also his cousin. Four died, however, leaving a daughter and two sons both of whom became musicians. Wilhelm Friedemann (1710–84)

was the eldest and one of the most distinguished of Johann
Sebastian's sons. The second son, Carl Philip Emanuel
(1714–88), possessed remarkable skill in improvisation, and
he wrote a large number of vocal and instrumental works,
including two oratorios. He was occasionally known as the
*Berlin* or *Hamburg* Bach. One year after Maria Barbara died in
1720, Johann Sebastian married Anna Magdalena Wulken
who bore him thirteen children, four daughters and nine sons
of whom only two became active musicians and composers.
Johann Christoph Friedrich (1732–95) was the eldest surviving son of Johann Sebastian's second marriage. He too was a
composer of some merit, his output including cantatas,
motets, symphonies, keyboard concertos, sonatas, chamber
music and songs. Johann Christian (1735–82) was the
youngest son of Johann Sebastian by his second wife. He
studied music under his father and subsequently under his
brother, Carl Philip Emanuel. He became known as the
*English* or *London* Bach, and he pioneered the use of the piano
as a solo instrument in Britain. His compositions included
eleven operas, an oratorio, over thirty piano concertos, more
than ninety symphonies, orchestral works, chamber music,
piano music and songs.

5  Eighty-eight.
6  Seventeen string quartets: op. 18 nos. 1–6 in F, G, D, C
minor, A and B flat; op. 59 nos. 1–3 in F, E minor and C (these
three quartets are nicknamed *Rasumovsky* as they were dedicated to the Count of that name who was a keen chamber music
player); op. 74 in E flat, *The Harp*; op. 95 in F minor; op. 127
in E flat; op. 130 in B flat; op. 131 in C sharp minor; op. 132 in
A minor; op. 133 *Grosse fuge* (originally composed as a finale
to op. 130); op. 135 in F.

Thirty-two piano sonatas: op. 2 nos. 1–3 in F minor, A and C;
op. 7 in E flat; op. 10 nos. 1–3 in C minor, F and D; op. 13 in C
minor, *Pathétique*; op. 14 nos. 1–2 in E and G; op. 22 in B flat;
op. 26 in A flat; op. 27 nos. 1–2 in E flat and C sharp minor,
*Moonlight*; op. 28 in D, *Pastoral*; op. 31 nos. 1–3 in G, D
minor, *Tempest* and E flat; op. 49 and nos. 1–2 in G minor and

G; op. 53 in C, *Waldstein*; op. 54 in F; op. 57 in F minor, *Appassionata*; op. 78 in F sharp; op. 79 in G; op. 81a in E flat, *Les Adieux*; op. 90 in G minor; op. 101 in A; op. 106 in B flat, *Hammerklavier*; op. 109 in E; op. 110 in A flat: op. 111 in C minor.

Nine symphonies: No. 1 in C, op. 21; No. 2 in D, op. 36; No. 3 in E flat, op. 55, *Eroica*; No. 4 in B flat, op. 60; No. 5 in C minor, op. 67; No. 6 in F, op. 68, *Pastoral*; No. 7 in A, op. 92; No. 8 in F, op. 93; No. 9 in D minor, op. 125, *Choral*. There is also a *Jena* Symphony since found to be composed by Friederich Witt, attributed to Beethoven and discovered at Jena in 1910, and the *Battle* Symphony, correctly known as *Wellington's Victory*. This was originally composed by Beethoven for the mechanical orchestra known as the Panharmonicon, invented by his friend Johann Mälzel (better known as the inventor of the metronome), who later urged Beethoven to re-score the work for conventional orchestra.

Seven concertos: Piano: No. 1 in C, op. 15 (really No. 2); No. 2 in B flat, op. 19 (really No. 1); No. 3 in C minor, op. 37; No. 4 in C, op. 58; No. 5 in E flat, op. 73, *Emperor*; Violin Concerto: op. 61 in D; Triple Concerto, op. 56 in C for pianoforte, violin and violoncello. N.B. The two piano concertos op. 15 and op. 19 are first period works; op. 19 (1795) was composed before the op. 15 (1798).

In addition to the above, Beethoven also composed the following: early Concerto in D (one movement only); Konzertstück, the manuscript of which was lost or it was never finished. There is also the Piano Concerto in D, which is an arrangement by Beethoven of his own Violin Concerto.

### The Odd One Out

1   Vincenzo Bellini (1801–35). Of these four composers chiefly famous for opera, Bellini alone wrote no chamber music. Giuseppe Verdi (1813–1901) wrote a String Quartet in E minor (1873) and Giacomo Puccini (1858–1924) composed *I*

*Crisantemi*, Scherzo, fugues, a String Quartet in D and a fragment of a piano trio. A String Quartet in D is the only surviving quartet of Gaetano Donizetti (1797–1848), although he wrote many for private performance in Bergamo.

2 *King Stephen*. This is an overture by Beethoven (op. 117), written in 1817; *King Priam* and *King Roger* are both operas, written by Michael Tippett (b. 1905) and Karol Szymanowski (1882–1937) respectively.

3 *Sea Pictures*. Debussy's *La Mer* and Handel's *Water Music* are both scored for orchestra; Elgar's *Sea Pictures* is scored for contralto voice with orchestra.

4 No. 37, K. 444. They are all numbers of Mozart symphonies, but Symphony No. 37 was written by Michael Haydn although Mozart did write a slow introduction to the work.

5 *St Nicholas*. This is a cantata by Benjamin Britten, while *St Paul* is an oratorio by Mendelssohn and *St Ludmilla* an oratorio by Dvořák.

6 Placido Domingo. Although all these musicians were born in Spain, Domingo is a famous tenor, while Nicanor Zabaleta and Marisa Robles are eminent harpists.

## The Pioneers

1 Joseph Lanner (1801–43). He was the leader of a quartet in which Johann Strauss, his subsequent rival, played the viola. The quartet later developed into an orchestra and both Lanner and Strauss wrote for it the waltzes, galops, quadrilles, polkas and marches that soon became popular throughout the world. Lanner eventually had 208 works published but left many scores unprinted.

2 Jacques Offenbach (1819–80). His music was immensely popular at the time and he was considered the foremost composer of light opera of his day, writing 102 stage works.

3 Hervé, real name Florimund Ronger (1825–92). He wrote over fifty operettas, a symphony and ballets, and although he was unquestionably the creator of the French operetta, he was later eclipsed by the brilliance of Offenbach.

4 Hector Berlioz (1803–69). In addition to many works that

were unique in advanced scoring technique for the time,
Berlioz also wrote a *Treatise on Instrumentation* that, for a
long time, held first place among works of its class.
5 Gottfried Silbermann (1683–1753). Initially an organ
   builder, he was famous as the first to manufacture a hammer-
   action pianoforte similar to that of Bartolemmeo Cristofori.
   Bach tried some of Silbermann's pianos during his visit to Frederick the Great.
6 Johann Strauss the elder (1793–1866). Both as a composer
   and conductor he and Lanner raised the level of dance music.
   He published some 152 waltzes, twenty-four galops, thirteen polkas, thirty-two quadrilles, six cotillons and contre-
   danses, eighteen marches and six potpourris. His son, Johann
   Strauss the younger, subsequently carried on the tradition
   and became known as 'the waltz king'.

## Variations on a Theme

1 Caprice No. 24 for unaccompanied violin; in all Brahms
  wrote twenty-eight variations on this Caprice.
2 A movement from Handel's Harpsichord Suite No. 5. The
  Air and Variations from this Harpsichord Suite are known as
  *The Harmonious Blacksmith*.
3 A theme from Henry Purcell's incidental music to the play
  *Abdelazar*, composed in 1695; the play was written by Aphra
  Benn.
4 The *Dies Irae* (*Day of Wrath*) from the plainsong Requiem
  Mass. The theme has also been used by many other composers
  including Granville Bantock (1868–1946), Peter Maxwell
  Davies (b. 1934), Anton Kraft (1749–1820), Nikolai Miaskovsky (1881–1950), Ottorino Respighi (1879–1936),
  Camille Saint-Saëns (1835–1921), Déodat de Sévérac (1872–
  1921), Kaikhosru Sorabji (b. 1892), Peter Ilich Tchaikovsky
  (1840–93) and Ralph Vaughan Williams (1872–1958).
5 'Baa baa black sheep', the tune known variously as 'Ah, vous
  dirai-je, Maman' and 'Twinkle, twinkle little star'.
6 The duet from Act 1 of Mozart's *Don Giovanni*, 'Là ci darem
  la mano'.

## Musical Terms

1 *Andante* means a moderate tempo—a walking pace—while *allegro* means lively but not very fast.

2 The direction *lento* means slow; *presto* is a fast speed, quicker than *allegro*.

3 *Diminuendo* is a direction to decrease the sound of the note, chord or phrase, while *crescendo* is a direction to increase its loudness.

4 Usually indicated by the sign *pp*, *pianissimo* means as softly as possible; *fortissimo*, which is usually indicated by the sign *ff*, means as loud as possible.

5 *Accelerando* means accelerating the pace; *rallentando* is slowing down the pace.

6 *Scherzando* means playfully or jokingly; *tremolando* is a fluctuation in intensity (as distinct from *vibrato*, which is a fluctuation in pitch).

# 14 WHO AND WHAT?

## What is the Difference?

1 Giacomo Puccini (1858–1924) was an Italian composer of many popular operas including *La Bohème* and *Madam Butterfly*. Nicola Piccini or Piccinni (1728–1800) was an Italian composer of over 120 forgotten operas including *La buona figliola* and *Iphigenia in Tauris*.
2 Johann, the elder (1804–49); Johann, the younger (1825–99); Joseph (1827–70); Eduard (1835–1916).
3 Clarino is a four-foot reed organ stop. A clarina is an instrument of the clarinet family, which was invented by Wagner for use in his operas.
4 Beethoven: Symphony No. 6 in F, op. 68, *Pastoral*; Handel: 'Pastoral Symphony' from *Messiah*; Vaughan Williams: Symphony No. 3, first performed in 1922.
5 Printed at the end of a section of music, attacca means go on immediately. Attacco is a short theme treated by imitation.
6 Beethoven: a setting of Goethe's poem for voice and orchestra, opus 112; Mendelssohn: an overture, opus 27.

## What is the Question?

1 What is a symphony?
2 Who was Dr Ludwig (Ritter von) Köchel?
3 What is an octave?
4 Can you give the numbers of the symphonies by Mozart that are entitled *Paris, Haffner, Linz, Prague* and *Jupiter*?
5 What are the names of the principal authentic ancient modes?
6 What are the titles applied to the symphonies by Haydn that are numbered No. 45 in F minor; No. 48 in C; No. 92 in G; No. 94 in G; No. 103 in E flat?

## Who Am I?

1  Arriaga (Juan Crisostomo Arriaga y Balzola).
2  Richard Strauss.
3  Niccolò Paganini.
4  Ignaz Moscheles.
5  Franz Liszt.
6  Clara Schumann.

## Who Said? (1)

1  Ludwig van Beethoven (1770–1827). In a letter to his friend and teacher, Ferdinand Ries, 22 December 1822.
2  Franz Liszt (1811–86). In a letter to Wilhelm von Lenz, 1852.
3  Franz Schubert (1791–1828). An entry in his diary, 13 June 1816.
4  Dmitri Tiompkin (b. 1899). Part of his acceptance speech for his academy award for the best original dramatic musical score, used in the film *The High and Mighty*, 1955.
5  Hector Berlioz (1803–69). Replying to his critics in *Les Grotesques de la Musique*, 1859.
6  Peter Ilich Tchaikovsky (1840–93). An excerpt from his diary for 1886.

## Who Said? (2)

1  Alphonse de Lamartine (1790–1869).
2  George Bernard Shaw in *Music in London*, 1890–4, and again in 1931.
3  Samuel Johnson (1709–84) in about 1776.
4  Ludwig van Beethoven. This passage is part of a remarkable letter written in Heiligenstadt, near Vienna, in 1802, after Beethoven realised that he was condemned to deafness. Known as the 'Heiligenstadt Testament', it was addressed to his brothers Caspar and Johann, and much of the statement is written as if it were a last message.
5  Sir Arthur Sullivan (1842–1900) in 1888.
6  Sir Thomas Beecham (1879–1961).

# SUGGESTED READING

If, after working your way through this book, you have been spurred to delve deeper into the highways and byways of music and the record industry, the following books might be of value.

*Collins Encyclopedia of Music*, Sir Jack Westrup and Frank Llewellyn Harrison, Collins, 1976
*Complete Opera Book*, Gustav Kobbé, Bodley Head, 1976
*The Concise Oxford Dictionary of Music* (second edition), Percy Scholes, Oxford University Press, 1968
*The Encyclopedia of Dance and Ballet*, Mary Clarke and David Vaughan (editors), Pitman, 1977
*The Encyclopedia of Opera*, Leslie Orrey, Pitman, 1976
*An Encyclopedia of Quotations about Music*, Nat Shapiro (editor), David & Charles, 1978
*Everyman's Dictionary of Music*, Eric Blom, Dent, 1974
*The Fabulous Phonograph*, Roland Gelatt, Cassell, 1977
*The 'Gramophone' Guide to Classical Composers and Recordings*, Lionel Salter (editor), Salamander Books, 1978
*International Music Guide*, Derek Elley (editor), Tantivy Press, issued annually
*More Opera Nights*, Ernest Newman, Putnam & Co, 1954
*The Music Goes Round and Round*, Peter Gammond, Quartet Books, 1980
*A New Dictionary of Music*, Arthur Jacobs, Penguin Books, 1970
*Opera Nights*, Ernest Newman, Putnam & Co, new edition, 1956
*The Oxford Companion to Music* (tenth edition), Percy Scholes, Oxford University Press, 1970
*The Penguin Stereo Record Guide*, Edward Greenfield, Robert Layton and Ivan March, Penguin Books, revised edition, 1977
*Wagner Nights*, Ernest Newman, Putnam & Co, 1968; Pan Books, 1977

In addition, the excellent *BBC Music Guides* should be mentioned; these are reasonably priced and authoritatively written.

There are also many excellent magazines, issued fortnightly and monthly, that are worth investigating, for example:

| | |
|---|---|
| *Classical Music Fortnightly* | *Music and Musicians* |
| *The E. M. G. Monthly Letter* | *The Musical Times* |
| *Gramophone* | *Opera* |
| *Hi Fi News and Record Review* | *Records and Recording* |